WADSWORTH PHILOSOPHERS SERIES

D0777398

ON

HUSSERL

Victor Velarde-Mayol
University of South Florida

Wadsworth
Thomson Learning.

Australia • Canada • Denmark • Japan • Mexico • New Zealand • Philippines
Puerto Rico • Singapore • Spain • United Kingdom • United States

To Susan

B3279
.H94
V45
2000
Cop. 2

9780534576103

Printed in the United States of America
  2 3 4 5 6 7 03 02 01 00

For permission to use material from this text, contact us:
Web: www.thomsonrights.com
Fax: 1-800-730-2215
Phone: 1-800-730-2214

For more information, contact:
Wadsworth/Thomson Learning
10 Davis Drive
Belmont, CA 94002-3098
USA
www.wadsworth.com

ISBN: 0-534-57610-9

Contents

Preface

To write an introductory book on Husserl's phenomenology is a real challenge. Any person, who has tried to read one of Husserl's works, would have noticed that not only writes at a high technical level, but also that he creates his own terminology. In writing an introductory book on Husserl, one is tempted to translate Husserl's technical expressions into a more palatable language, but this task is almost impossible without betraying Husserl's intentions. Husserl dedicated an enormous quantity of time to polishing and defining the terminology used pervasively in his works, mostly technical words coined for concepts that were new at that time. So, my challenge is to keep Husserl's terminology and at the same time bring his philosophy to people who are not familiar with his thought.

In writing this book I had two main guiding ideas, first, a view of Husserl's philosophical development, and, second, to offer some of Husserl's philosophical analysis as a positive contribution to human knowledge. I think that Husserl's analysis of mental acts is still useful, and this is something that current philosophy of mind has not exploited thoroughly. Husserl's analysis on truth and evidence are, I believe, masterpieces of philosophy. Nevertheless, most of the expositions about Husserl in our days dedicate too much space to the last period of Husserl's phenomenology, with the inevitable bypassing or overlooking of the first period of his phenomenology. In this book I wanted to correct this trend, and I dedicated a good portion of the book to Husserl's analysis of intentionality as founded in his *Logical Investigations*.

This book is divided into four chapters. The first is an exposition of Husserl's philosophical formation, his origins and influence. The second chapter is Husserl's analysis of mental acts in *Logical Investigations*, with the intention of offering to the public one of the most brilliant analyses of consciousness: the distinction between matter and quality of mental acts, and the theory of truth and evidence. The third chapter is an exposition of the phenomenological method, and how the method became a philosophy of consciousness. The last chapter is a short presentation of the main subjects of the last period of

1

Husserl's phenomenology, his phenomenological-transcendental idealism, the notion of the constitution of the intentional object, the egology, his investigations on intersubjectivity, and finally, one of the most interesting ideas in Husserl's philosophy, namely, the life-world.

The logical exposition of Husserl's phenomenology is by starting with the phenomenological method, but I preferred to follow the historical order and how Husserl arrived to a clear idea of the method. The second chapter is based mostly in *Logical Investigations*, and it assumes that the reader knows the phenomenological method, which Husserl is using. But it is only years later, when Husserl decides to clarify and develop the method he used pervasively in earlier works.

1

Philosophical Development

1. Years of Formation

Edmund Husserl was born in Prossnitz (Moravia) on April 8, 1859. (At that time, Prossnit belonged to the Austro-Hungarian Empire, today it is part of the Czech Republic.) Husserl was raised in a Jewish family, although with indifference for its religion. During the first years of school, Husserl did not stand out as a good student, as a matter of fact, the principal commented that Husserl was the worst student of the School.

Husserl went to the University of Leipzig (Germany) for two years (1876-1878) to study mathematics, physics, astronomy and introductory courses of philosophy. At that time, Husserl met Thomas Masaryk —a disciple of the philosopher Franz Brentano— who was to be president of Czechoslovakia. Masaryk convinced Husserl to study philosophy. Thus, Husserl studied Descartes, British Empiricism, Leibniz, and Berkeley.

During the next three years (1878-1881), Husserl continued his mathematical studies at the University of Berlin with the prestigious mathematicians Kronecker (in Theory of Numbers) and Weierstrass (in Analysis). During this time, Husserl became interested in works such as Hobbes' *De Cive*, A. Bain's *Mind and Body*, Spinoza's *Ethica*, and some works of Schopenhauer. In 1881 Husserl moved to the University of Vienna, where he obtained his doctorate in mathematics with his dissertation on the theory of variations. During his military service (1883-1884), Husserl read Hegel's *Phenomenology of Spirit*, and some works of Aristotle and H. Spencer.

Husserl's real philosophical conversion occurred under the influence of the philosopher Franz Brentano.[1] Husserl attended Brentano's lectures on descriptive and phenomenological psychology during 1884-1885, and continued under the mentoring of Brentano until 1886. From Brentano's lectures Husserl realized that philosophy was a science, and a rigorous science that was the basis of the rest of the sciences. During this time, under the guidance of Brentano,

3

Husserl became involved in the study of Hume's philosophy and E. Mach's analysis of sensations. Husserl learned from Brentano the potential of a full analysis of the intentionality of mental acts. In fact, the discovery of phenomenology years later started as a sophistication of Brentano's analysis of intentionality that is found in Brentano's lectures of 1884-5, and published under the title of *Descriptive Psychology*.

The relationship between Husserl and Brentano was more than academic, there was a sincere friendship and admirable disciple-professor relationship. Years later, when Brentano exiled himself to Florence (Italy), Husserl visited him, and —Husserl recalled— he could not help but show gratitude and veneration for this genial and eminent philosopher and master who was Brentano. At the same time Husserl felt like a shy beginner in front of Brentano who still exercised a very strong influence over Husserl. Nevertheless, at that time, both philosophers had different opinions on what philosophy should be regarding important issues. While Brentano became a strong empiricist (what is called Brentano's Reism), Husserl was developing his phenomenology with a strong touch of idealism. So, Husserl sadly recalls that there was no agreement between the phenomenological method that Husserl was developing and Brentano's philosophy.[2] Probably, Brentano's strong empiricism could not find a common ground with Husserl's orientation toward idealism, abstract entities, universals, and ideal beings. One has to take into consideration that Brentano's first attacks were against German Idealism, and later Brentano radicalized these attacks in what is called "Reism," the doctrine that there are only things and nothing more than things (no universals, no abstract entities, etc.).

2. Period of Logicism

Husserl obtained an academic position at the University of Halle, where he remained for about fourteen years (1887-1901.) Before awarding an academic position, it is the procedure in German universities to confirm the doctorate with a thesis (thesis of habilitation), which Husserl defended before the academic tribunal composed of the professors C. Stumpf (one of the main disciples of Brentano), G. Cantor (one of the most important mathematicians of the century), and Knoblauch, who examined Husserl in philosophy, mathematics and physics. Husserl presented his thesis on "The Concept of Number." Thus, Husserl completed the first step in becoming a university professor (*Privatdozent*).

The first years of Husserl's academic activity were dedicated

4

mainly to philosophy of mathematics. The first important result of this was the publication in 1891 of *"Philosophy of Arithmetic,"* with the subtitle *"Psychological and Logical Investigations,"*[3] dedicated to his master Brentano. In this work, Husserl studied the foundations of numbers and operations with numbers. Husserl's method was borrowed from a variation of Brentano's technique: the metaphysical analysis of wholes and parts, and descriptive psychology. Husserl tried to answer the question of how a number is given to us when there is no presentation or intuition of a number. Although Husserl was familiar with Frege's criticism of John Stuart Mill's psychologism, and mentioned Frege very often, Frege felt that Husserl's analysis in *Philosophy of Arithmetic* was influenced by psychologism, that is to say, Husserl seemed to derive mathematical laws from psychological laws. Even though *Philosophy of Arithmetic* was a highly scholarly work on the foundations of mathematics with very interesting insights for this field, it was not yet a phenomenological work, but it contained many topics that Husserl would use later.

Husserl's first phenomenological work was *Logical Investigations*, which he began to write in 1890, and which was published during the years 1900-1901 in two volumes. The first volume —"Prolegomena to Pure Logic"— was published when Husserl was still a *Privatdozent*. Here, Husserl turned to a strong logicism and against any kind of psychologism. This volume deals with the pure logic, and is a sharp criticism against scepticism and relativism. Years later, in 1906, Husserl wrote in his diary: "I have been through enough torments from lack of clarity and from doubt that wavers back and forth ... Only one need absorbs me: I must win clarity, else I cannot live; I cannot bear life unless I can believe that I shall achieve it."[4] The need for clarity and certainty was an important element in the development of phenomenology, and it accompanied Husserl throughout his life. The first manifestation of the need for certainty was the criticism of psychologism, which was a form of relativism. The positive result of Husserl's criticism against relativism and psychologism was the idea of a pure logic.

The second volume is divided into six investigations, in which Husserl studies the theory of meaning, universals, the theory of whole and parts, the idea of a pure grammar, the analysis of the intentional acts, and, finally, a theory of categories.

In 1901, Husserl was named extraordinary professor of the University of Göttingen, ending his period at the University of Halle with three important publications: *On the Concept of Number*, *Philosophy of Arithmetic*, and *Logical Investigations*, the latter opened the horizon for a new future for philosophy —phenomenology.

5

3. Maturation of Phenomenology

3.1. The years at the University of Göttingen

Husserl developed and culminated his phenomenology during his years at the University of Göttingen (1901-1916). In this period, he was in contact with the mainstream philosophical schools, mainly neo-Kantianism (P. Natorp, H. Rickert, E. Cassirer, etc.) and the School of Graz created by A. Meinong. As a matter of fact, Husserl studied Meinong's theory of objects, and probably used some elements of Meinong's notion of pure object and the theory of assumptions to elaborate what Husserl termed "phenomenological reduction."

Already in 1905, Husserl felt confident that his phenomenology had arrived to a secure position, and he believed that the phenomenological method was the answer for a philosophy as a rigorous science. Although the dependence on Brentano's phenomenological psychology is obvious, (and Husserl recognizes this) he thought that his phenomenology was better understood as a continuation of the philosophical problems posed by Plato, Kant and Hume. In fact, Husserl planned to write an extensive work on the critique of reason, which he never finished.

Husserl's philosophy was not only well-known among philosophers in Europe, but through his disciples his influence started to spread throughout Germany and outside. Nevertheless, in 1905, the faculty of the University of Göttingen rejected the promotion of Husserl to the position of ordinary professor. Just a year later, the faculty reluctantly promoted Husserl to this position.

In these years, Husserl published two major works, "*Philosophy as a Rigorous Science*" (1910) and what is considered a detailed explanation of the phenomenological method, "*Ideas Pertaining to a Pure Phenomenology and to a Phenomenological Philosophy*" (1913). The latter was published in the first volume of the official periodical publication of the phenomenological movement (*Jahrbuch für Philosophie und phänomenologische Forschung*), which was established with Moritz Geiger, Alexander Pfänder, Adolf Reinach, and Husserl as the chief editor.

In *Ideas*, Husserl not only presents a method of philosophizing, but also a philosophy, which some disciples do not consider to be ontologically neutral (as Husserl claimed), namely, a transcendental phenomenology. When Husserl published *Ideas*, many disciples abandoned Husserl's project of a transcendental phenomenology. They felt that Husserl was betraying the neutrality of his phenomenological method in favor of a problematic phenomenological idealism. They

6

believed that Husserl's motto "to the things themselves" in his earlier work, *Logical Investigations*, had been abandoned. Husserl resented this bitterly.

In reality, it was in the lectures of the summer semester of 1907 that Husserl made the change and turned from the view of *Logical Investigations* to that of *Ideas*. These lectures are published in the posthumous work "*The Idea of Phenomenology*." In these lectures one can see subjects that are familiar in *Ideas*, namely, the idea of a transcendental phenomenology and a phenomenology of constituting consciousness.

During these years, many disciples gathered around Husserl and formed the Göttingen Circle. The main characteristic of this group was its interest in phenomenology as a descriptive method of essences by means of the eidetic reduction. The basic text used by this group was still Husserl's *Logical Investigations*. The philosophical work of this group was outstanding, which allowed the incipient phenomenology to grow fast and deep. But most of the work was rooted in a conception of phenomenology as a mere method (this was the original plan in *Logical Investigations.*)[5] This explains the resistance of this group to Husserl's evolution to a transcendental phenomenology in *Ideas*, in which phenomenology is more than a method.

Philosophers who belonged to the Göttingen Circle were, for example, A. Reinach (who developed a phenomenology of ethics, religion, and right), D. von Hildebrand and Max Scheler (who were interested in a phenomenology of ethics), A. Koyrè (who worked in the history of science), Edith Stein and H. Conrad-Martius (who developed a metaphysics based on phenomenology). Two of the most brilliant disciples, Reinach and Stein, died in their earlier careers. Reinach was a casualty of war (1917), and Stein died in the concentration camp of Auschwitz.

Husserl's last year in Göttingen was painful. He suffered the loss of many disciples, friends, and even one son in the World War I. The suffering of this year and the atrocities of the war had a strong impact on Husserl's thought.

3.2. The Years at the University of Freiburg

The year in which his son died, Husserl was appointed at the University of Freiburg as the successor of the neo-Kantian philosopher H. Rickert. Husserl spent from 1916 to 1928 at the University of Freiburg. In this period he wrote two major and very important works for the understanding of phenomenology: *Formal and Transcendental Logic* and *Cartesian Meditations*. One of the most interesting characteristics of this period is the universalization of movement of phenomenology, especially in France, Czechoslovakia, England, Japan, and the United States. Husserl wrote some papers for the Japanese periodical publication *Kaizo*. This event explains the interest in phenomenology in Japan to this day.

Philosophically, Husserl became interested in the monadology developed by one of his disciples (D. Mahnke), which became the metaphysical orientation of phenomenology, but from the point of view of phenomenological idealism. This marks sharply Husserl's attempt to go beyond a phenomenological method to a philosophical phenomenology, a phenomenology with metaphysical content. In *Ideas I* and *Cartesian Meditations*, Husserl maintains that it is futile to pursue a method without a goal. Every method needs a destination to which the method is directed. So, the original plan of phenomenology as a pure method was abandoned at this stage of Husserl's philosophical development. Phenomenology became a method with its own content.

In his new plan for phenomenology, Husserl distinguished between (i) a transcendental phenomenology, and (ii) a universal philosophical phenomenology or first philosophy. (i) Transcendental phenomenology has the goal to investigate the most basic concepts of science and spontaneous knowledge, and (ii) the universal philosophical phenomenology, or first philosophy, deals with the traditional subjects of philosophy.

Husserl tried to write down all these ideas in a great systematic work, something in the line of the *Sumae* of the medieval times, an exhaustive exposition of phenomenology, its method and subjects, but the difficulties of a work of such a magnitude kept Husserl from completing it. Instead, Husserl had to be content with less ambitious works, but still masterpieces of philosophy such as *Phenomenology of Inner Time Consciousness* (1928) and *Formal and Transcendental Logic* (1929), which is one of the milestones of phenomenology, and, according to many scholars, is considered the most representative and finished work of Husserl and phenomenology. Very probably, Husserl considered *Formal and Transcendental Logic* the most substantial work written by him, although he said explicitly that *Cartesian Meditations* was the main work of his life. Probably, he referred to the achievements the latter book dealt with, namely, a clear exposition of the phenomenological method and its philosophical problems. In some way, *Cartesian Meditations* is a complement of *Formal and Transcendental Logic*, especially on the subject of intersubjectivity as a possible starting point to escape from the solipsism into which the phenomenological ideals seemed to slip. If the conscious ego is a monad, a close unity *a la Leibniz*, the danger of falling into solipsism is immediate. Because of this, Husserl had to develop a phenomenological theory of intersubjectivity. However, this project is incomplete because a full development of an effective phenomenological intersubjectivity of the ego as a monad is missing. Perhaps, one of the most problematic issues in Husserl's phenomenology of intersubjectivity is the passing from an immanent philosophy (the phenomenology of *Ideas*) into a philosophy of transcendence, in which other egos are recognized. All these problems are dispersed in numerous manuscripts under the title of "Phenomenology of Intersubjectivity."[6]

Many disciples gathered together around Husserl forming what was called the Circle of Freiburg, which certainly contributed greatly to the movement of phenomenology. Among the outstanding disciples belonging to this group were M. Heidegger (philosophy of existence), E. Fink, and L. Landgrebe (metaphysics), who were, in addition, assistant professors with Husserl. Other disciples, were H. G. Gadamer (Hermeneutics), E. Levinas (ethics), J. P. Sartre (existentialism), etc. It is interesting to note that Husserl saw in Heidegger the continuation of the phenomenological tradition. This is the reason Husserl allowed him to have access to all his manuscripts; Husserl even entrusted Heidegger with the publication of *Phenomenology of Inner Time Consciousness*, and later Husserl facilitated the way to a professorship as his successor. Nevertheless, Husserl realized later that both philosophers had quite different philosophies in basic and important points. Probably, the disciple who was more closest to Husserl's ideas was E. Fink, to the extent that Fink developed his own phenomenological investigations under the direction and supervision of Husserl.

Of some interest for the history of philosophy, I will mention two things: (1) in 1922 (June), Husserl gave a series of important lectures in London, where he met G.E. Moore. (2) It is interesting to notice, that Rudolf Carnap attended Husserl's lectures during the academic years of 1924-25. The influence of Husserl in Carnap is uncertain (probably some of Husserl's ideas about pure logic), but what is clear is that Carnap followed the opposite positions to Husserl, the logical positivism.

4. The Last Period of Husserl's Philosophy

What is considered by some scholars to be the last period of Husserl's philosophy (1928-1939)—he years in Freiburg after his retirement (March 31, 1928)—is characterized mainly by the turn of phenomenology into a phenomenology of the life-world, which is found in *The Crisis of European Sciences and the Transcendental Phenomenology*.

The motivations that triggered this work were the negative circumstances that surrounded German philosophy, and Western culture, in general. Husserl felt the social damage that a deep crisis of knowledge was causing. Husserl made public these worries in his answer to Heidegger's homage (*Festschrift*) to him on his 70th birthday (April 8, 1929): "I had the necessity to philosophize; otherwise, I couldn't have lived in this world."[7] Husserl's interest was not only to denounce the deplorable state of philosophy, and as a result, science and human culture in general, in his time, but also the challenge that his listeners had to overcome it, and to give positive solutions.

During this period, Husserl's interests seemed to take a different turn, which resulted in a departure from his more Cartesian based philosophy of thirty years of phenomenological research to another more occupied with history and the world of life. This is seen by some scholars as a rupture. Nevertheless, however innovative this view is, Husserl maintained a very consistent line of thought not only with *Ideas* and *Cartesian Meditations*, but also with his earlier phenomenological work, *Logical Investigations*.

At this time, the divergences between Husserl and Heidegger were enormous. This disagreement can be seen en several occasions: (i) First, after the impact of Heidegger's *Being and Time* in philosophical circles, Husserl read carefully Heidegger's work, and was deeply disappointed; (ii) but especially the failure to write jointly an article of introduction to phenomenology for the *Encyclopaedia Britannica* was very damaging for the professional relationship between both philosophers. (iii) When Heidegger wrote *What is Metaphysics?*, Husserl's objection to Heidegger became overtly public. Explicitly, Husserl said that (a) there is a definitive incompatibility between both ways of philosophizing, (b) although Heidegger's philosophy is certainly deep and in some ways genial, it is also completely unscientific: "a genial unscientific philosophy." (c) Heidegger based his philosophy in a gross misunderstanding of phenomenology, especially in the notion of phenomenon and its relation to ontology; and (d) Heidegger's philosophy is what Husserl tried to object to and fight all his career: unfounded statements, and, as a consequence, it is not a rigorous philosophy. Husserl, under the strong influence of his master Brentano, conceived of philosophy as a rigorous science, which is the main task of phenomenology. Husserl saw in Heidegger's thought not only a dangerous relativism and pragmatism that could damage the good sense of a scientific mind, but also a mere ideology, which is incompatible with what a scientific philosophy should be: a philosophy without presuppositions, without dogmatisms.

Between 1929 and 1934, Husserl tried to develop the phenomenology of intersubjectivity that was initiated in the fifth *Cartesian Meditations*. The original plan was a great systematic work, but he could not finish it. The result was an interesting and daring metaphysics: a monadological universe of egos. Between 1934 and 1937, Husserl dedicated his efforts to the preparation of *The Crisis*. Husserl's plan was to create a general introduction to the phenomenological philosophy as a substitution for his failure to write a great systematic work.

In November of 1933, the faculty of philosophy of the University of Southern California in Los Angeles offered a chair to Husserl. Husserl did not accept it, probably he felt that the few years of life he might have left would be better dedicated to write and make the revisions to his unpublished writings.

In 1936 (January 15th), the German Government (under the Nazi regime) withdrew Husserl's teaching license due to his Jewish condition. Under the adverse circumstances, Heidegger advised Husserl to flee from Germany. Meanwhile, Heidegger was named rector of the University of Freiburg.

In 1937 Husserl became seriously ill, and died on April 27, 1938, in Freiburg im Breisgau.

Most of Husserl's writings were not published during his life. Husserl commented that the most important part of his work was in manuscripts (the published works during Husserl's lifetime were only a fraction of his entire writings.) What is now the Husserl Archives is located in Lovaina (Belgium), under the direction of P.H.L. van Breda, who saved Husserl's manuscripts from destruction during World War II.

5. The Idea of Phenomenology

The original maxim of phenomenology was the motto: "back to things themselves." This expression has many meanings. (1) It originally indicated a return to what is objective (logical, ethical, etc.) as an object of consciousness (intentional object). (2) Another meaning is a reaction against Hume's empiricism and Kant's transcendental idealism. (3) But maybe, the meaning that played originally an extensive role was a reaction against scepticism and relativism, which rejected the idea of a universal objectivity.[8]

The main objective of Husserl's philosophy was to establish the foundation for a radical and universal knowledge in confrontation with the growing scepticism that manifested scientific positivism and its

11

philosophical derivations. Philosophy was for Husserl a science that began from the ultimate foundation. Philosophy is a radical science because it is a science of the roots of all our knowledge (radical comes from the word "root"). Husserl tried to radicalize the foundations of human knowledge to make it immune to scepticism.

In order to achieve this task, Husserl conceived of a method—phenomenology—which is an analysis of everything that is given to our knowledge. What is given to our knowledge is called "phenomenon," which comes from Greek "phainomenon," meaning appearance. Husserl uses the term "phenomenon" in this sense. So, what is given to our knowledge is an appearance of something, what appears to me, a phenomenon. In this sense, phenomenology is the science of phenomena, of what is given or appears to our knowledge. This method is purely descriptive: phenomenology is the description of what is given to our knowledge. For example, consider the perception of a tree. A phenomenological analysis of this could be a description of what I see and understand in my perception of the tree, and what I see are colors, shapes, etc., and what I understand is that these colors and shapes are put together under the idea of tree. Hence, we can define provisionally the phenomenological method in the following way:

> Phenomenology = The method for the description and analysis of consciousness and what is given to consciousness, through which philosophy becomes a strict science.

The main idea behind this method is to avoid metaphysical constructions. In this sense, the motto "back to things themselves" means an opposition to constructions, premature systematization. "Back to things themselves" means to go to the immediate data given to me.

Phenomenology is not interested in facts, singular facts, but in essences, the ideas and universals. So, in describing the data given to consciousness, Husserl's phenomenological method tries to describe what is constant, essential, in these data. Thus, phenomenology is a science of the universal and necessary as far as what is essential is something necessary. For example, if the essence or idea of being human is the capability of being rational, then, it is necessary that rationality is a property of the idea or essence of human being.

The phenomenological method seems to make a Kantian-like synthesis between the opposition of empiricism —based on observation— and rationalism —based on reason and a system of concepts in order to describe the structures of the experiential life. Husserl claims that there is no philosophical problem outside the scope of phenomenology because before becoming a problem it has to be given to my knowledge as a phenomenon for my consciousness, and phenomenology is precisely this, a descriptive analysis of what is given (a phenomenon) to our knowledge.

Husserl understood phenomenology in two ways, with one leading to the other: (a) Phenomenology as a philosophical method, and (b) phenomenology as a philosophical system. In the beginning of phenomenology (for example, in *Logical Investigations*), Husserl conceived of phenomenology as a method of analysis. Later, in *Ideas*, Husserl conceived of phenomenology as both a method and systematic philosophy, which he called "transcendental phenomenology." The phenomenological method leads to the philosophical system, but many disciples of Husserl rejected the idea that such an insightful philosophical method, with so many potentialities, ended up in another philosophical system.

The fascinating thing about phenomenology as a method is that it is not only for philosophical use, it also could be used in science. Psychiatry, for example, was enriched with the phenomenological analysis of what is happening in an altered consciousness, how a person with a depression perceives time, space, etc. Phenomenology was also applied to social sciences, economy, etc.

In the next chapter (Ch.2) we will see how Husserl applies the phenomenological method in *Logical Investigations* (1900-1901) without having formulated it explicitly; in Chapter 3, we will see how Husserl, with the publication of *Ideas* (1913), formulated explicitly the phenomenological method; Chapter 4 is dedicated to the application of the phenomenological and the derivation of phenomenology to a first philosophy, namely, a transcendental phenomenology, which is labeled by some scholars as another form of idealism. Here, Husserl made important modifications to the phenomenological method. If phenomenology was up to here a descriptive method, now it will be extended to a genetic method, in which the history of consciousness is used as an important tool to complete the phenomenology of consciousness. The last chapter deals with a new concept in phenomenology, the notion of life-world as the foundation of meaning, sciences, and human culture. Husserl introduces this concept in *Crisis* (1936), and it establishes a departure from his original positions according to some phenomenologists, but probably is just an enhancement of the traditional subjects of phenomenology.

Although the development of Husserl's philosophy is more complicated and intricate, it is illuminating to summarize his philosophical development in five consecutive steps steps: psychologism (*Philosophy of Arithmetic*), logical essentialism (*Logical Investigations*), transcendental idealism (*Ideas, Cartesian Meditations*, etc.), and finally, a phenomenology of life-world (*Crisis*).

ENDNOTES

[1] Cf. Boer, Th. de, *The Development of Husserl's Thought*, The Hague, M. Nijhoff, 1978.

[2] Cf. Schuhmann, K., *Husserl-Chronik. Denk- und Lebensweg Edmund Husserls*, The Hague, M. Nijhoff, 1977.

[3] Cf. Edmund Husserl, *Philosophie der Arithmetik. Psychologie und logische Untersuchungen*, in *Husserliana*, volume XII, pp. 1-283.

[4] H. Speigelberg, *The Phenomenological Movement*, The Hague, Martinus Nijhoff, 1965, quote in p. 82.

[5] Cf. Speigelberg, *The Phenomenological Movement*, pp. 168-227.

[6] Cf. *Husserliana*, vol. XIII-XV.

[7] K. Schumann, *Husserl-Chronik. Denk- und Lebensweg Edmund Husserls*, The Hague, M. Nijhoff, 1977, p.344.

[8] See the interesting study of Josef Seifert, *Back to Things in Themselves. A Phenomenological Foundation for Classical Realism*, New York, Routledge & Kegan Paul, 1987, pp 7-76..

2
Intentional Analysis

1. Introduction

In this chapter, we will see some ideas of Husserl's philosophy of arithmetic to pass to what triggered the beginning of phenomenology, the critique of psychologism. But the main section of this chapter will be the analysis of intentionality as stated in *Logical Investigations*. Specifically we will see in some detail the phenomenology of meaning, the analysis of the intentional act, the analysis of the phenomenon of truth, and the notion of categorial intuition.

The road to phenomenology starts from a clarification of the notion of science. Husserl, first, was interested in the philosophy of mathematics, later in the science of logic, and finally, arriving to phenomenology as a rigorous science. Husserl's first interest in phenomenology was as a method of establishing a foundation for the most abstract sciences, viz., mathematics and logic. Later, his phenomenological interest shifted into the subjective life of cognition and its correlative objects. This development explains the division of this chapter: philosophy of arithmetic, and anti-psychologism, on one hand, and pure logic, and the analysis of intentionality, on the other hand.

2. Philosophy of Arithmetic

In the first phase of development, phenomenology is mainly the science of the psychological origins of mathematics (arithmetic and geometry), and formal logic. Husserl goes from positions that resemble psychologism into an anti-psychologism and logicism.

Before we begin an analysis of the anti-psychologism as founded in *Logical Investigations*, it is interesting to review very briefly what Husserl accomplished in his *Philosophy of Arithmetic* (1891) This work was easily rejected and overlooked by many Husserlian scholars because of Frege's criticism. Frege labeled Husserl's work as psychologism, because of the derivation of mathematical notion from psychological laws. This criticism had a devastating effect for many

15

phenomenologists, who were inclined to see the work immature or unimportant. This reputation of Husserl's *Philosophy of Arithmetic* lasted until recent years. Nevertheless, a better study of this work reveals that the accusation of psychologism is inaccurate, and that it is a valuable scholarly work of enduring importance. The fact that Husserl later distanced himself from some theses of this work, does not mean that Husserl accepted Frege's criticism, as some scholars believed. Husserl's modification of some earlier theses had nothing to do with Frege's objections but very likely with the new orientation of Husserl's philosophy toward a phenomenology.

Husserl's objective in his *Philosophy of Arithmetic* is both an analysis of the basic concepts assumed in arithmetic (the concepts of plurality, unity and number) and a logical analysis of the symbolic methods used in arithmetic (the symbolic representation of numbers.) The ideas used by Husserl in this investigation came mainly from Brentano's descriptive psychology, and the mathematician Weierstrass. The following are some the main ideas of Husserl's work:[1]

(1) The clarification of any concept is made by determining the psychological origin. Because arithmetic is primarily a calculation, specifically, a calculation with cardinal numbers, Husserl is concerned with the psychological origins of the operation of calculating cardinal numbers.

(2) The logic origin of arithmetic is restricted to the symbolic representation of numbers. Following Brentano, Husserl distinguishes between two kinds of representations, intuitive representation in which the object represented is itself given, and symbolic representation in which the object (for example, a number) is represented only by a symbol. Here we do not have an intuition of the number. Nevertheless, symbolic representations presuppose in some way an intuitive representation. Now, not all arithmetic calculation deals with intuitive representation, for our intuitive grasp has important psychological limitations to a relatively small group of numbers (maybe the first natural numbers) in comparison to the unlimited series of numbers. So, Husserl thinks, most arithmetical calculations are made with symbolic representations.

(3) Number concepts (not the number itself) have their origin in psychological processes made by acts of collective combination. Frege interpreted this as psychologism, [2] and it is possible that Frege was right, but very probably what Husserl did was to offer a theory of the origin of the *concept* of number using the distinction between intuitive and symbolic representations. He did not offer a theory of the origin of the numbers themselves but a theory of the origin of the concept of number. So, his procedure is not a psychologization of numbers.

When Husserl dealt with the numbers themselves, he could not arrive to any solution of their origins because he could not reconcile the psychological process involved in the arithmetical operations—which are subjective in character— with the logic of numbers, which are objective in character.

Under the influence of the mathematician Hilbert, Husserl arrived to the conclusion that arithmetic could not begin with cardinal numbers, this change of mind implied another important change, namely, the abandonment of the operational theory of arithmetic developed in Husserl's *Philosophy of Arithmetic*, and the adoption of the new trend of an axiomatic theory of mathematics. This change of mind does not have to do with Frege's criticism, and the alleged psychologism, but with an internal process of understanding the foundations of mathematics.

3. Critique of Psychologism and Pure Logic

The first volume of *Logical Investigations* (1900) is entitled "Prolegomena to Pure Logic," and it has the main goal of introducing the science of pure logic, by which philosophy regains its own domain of research independent of psychology and any natural science. Having this in mind, the first task of *Logical Investigations* is to defend logic against psychologism and relativism. Most of the antipsychologistic arguments are built on two ideas: (i) Any theory denying the possibility of objectively true knowledge cannot avoid relativism; and relativism is a form of scepticism; (ii) The radical distinction between logic and psychology, a distinction that will be justified with the distinction between psychological act (intentional act) and intentional object.

3.1. Antipsychologism

What triggered the research and most of the inspiration of *Logical Investigations* was the refutation of logical psychologism. This refutation would clear the way to a general theory of science or pure logic, and to the analysis of intentionality (second part of *Logical Investigations*). The expression "logical psychologism" is used by Husserl to refer to the doctrine that derives logical laws from psychological laws, and confuses logic with regulative natural laws. In this confusion, psychologism talks about logic as "laws of thought" in such a way that a logical law is a natural law that regulates our thoughts.

Husserl saw with good insight that the main confusion that psychologism commits is a "metábasis eis állo génos" (a Greek expression meaning a change of genus, or what Ryle would say "a categorical mistake"). The metábasis of psychologism consists of transforming an ideal law (logic) into a real law (a physical or psychical law), a normative regulation into a causal regulation, a logical necessity into a real necessity.[3] The consequence of this confusion is that psychologism is unable to ground the absolute necessity of logical laws and thus ending in skepticism. Husserl offers several arguments to prove the gross mistake of psychologism.[4]

(1) Logical laws have absolute validity, while natural laws have merely probable validity. Psychological laws are vague generalizations of experience; they are assertions concerning approximate regularities in the coexistence or succession of matters of fact. This vagueness is shared by all laws of nature. Psychological laws, as every natural law, can never attain more than a *probable* validity. This is due to the nature of the object of a natural science. A natural science investigates causal connections of matter of fact, and these connections rest upon inductive generalizations of empirical data. This implies that psychological laws do not have absolute validity under all circumstances, or better, psychology is unable to exclude the possible falsification of its laws. On the contrary, logical laws demand absolute validity under all circumstances, in other words, logical laws are independent of all matter-of-fact circumstances. For example, the principle of contradiction claims an absolute validity in all circumstances, and a case that is not under the principle of contradiction is unthinkable.[5]

(2) Logical laws are not the cause of mental thinking. Logical laws do not regulate the psychological process of thinking as the laws of nature regulate natural phenomena (or more specifically, as the psychological laws regulate psychological processes). Logical laws regulate our thinking but they do not cause our thinking as psychological laws do.

The laws of logic are absolute in character; that is to say, they are valid at all times, for every person who understands them, and under all circumstances. This absolute character of logic is because logic does not refer to matters of fact and does not come from inductive generalizations of matter of fact. Natural laws are inductive generalizations from experience, and they are valid only under certain circumstances. The psychological process of thinking is a matter of fact; so, logical laws are not laws of psychological thinking as psychological laws are.[6]

Husserl makes interesting comparisons between logic and a calculator or computer. Certainly there are some common elements between the psychological performance of the thinking process and the physical performance of the functioning of a calculator.[7] The mechanical production of results in a calculator is regulated directly by physical laws, that is to say, by laws of nature (which are probable in character) in a manner that accords with the arithmetical laws. Now, Husserl rightly points out, "in order to explain the functioning of the machine in physical terms, no one will appeal to the arithmetical rather than the mechanical laws."[8] One may apply this idea to the psychological process of thinking. The psychological functioning of thinking is caused by the psychological laws and regulated but never caused by logical laws.

(3) Logical laws do not depend on the make-up of human nature. This logical relativism is called by Husserl "specific relativism" of logic, which is a form of anthropological relativism. Husserl's objection is that for this kind of relativism, logical laws are laws of thinking as a specific law of nature for humans, and as a consequence, logical laws may claim no eternity or atemporality at all (or as Husserl puts it, there is no ideal identity). If logical laws depend on the make-up of human nature, an alteration of this make-up, say, because of evolution, or the possibility of another rational species, will imply that logical laws are altered as well.[9]

This relativism, like any other, ends in a radical skepticism, which is unstable. Husserl points out that the anthropological foundation of logical laws runs "counter to the self-evident conditions for the possibility of a theory in general."[10] Now, a theory that negates the very conditions for the possibility of a theory in general ends up itself in "an evident contradiction between the sense of its own thesis and that which cannot with good sense be separated from any thesis as such."[11]

Husserl proves the absurdity of the specific relativism or logical anthropologism in the following way. (i) The same content of judgement or proposition can be true for one which belongs to the species *homo*, but false for another which belongs to a different species. (ii) Yet, the same content of a judgement or proposition cannot be both true and false in the same sense, for "what is true is absolutely and inherently true."[12]

In summary, psychologism is a relativization of logical laws to the specific make-up of psychological laws; and because psychological laws are conditioned and refutable by a possible experience, they cannot be the source for the absolute validity of the laws of logic.

3.2. The Idea of a Pure Logic

From Aristotle until now, logicians generally hold that formal logic is a pure science. A pure science means that it has nothing to do

19

with factual matters. So, formal logic is a science that is neither based on nor refers to factual matters. From here, the realm of logic is considered to have nothing to do with experience or the constitution of the world. Both experience and the actual constitution of the world are factual realms. It is believed among most of the logicians (maybe Quine is an exception) that logic, which is occupied with formal relations between objects, is said to be necessary. The necessity of logic means that the denial of any logical claim constitutes a self-contradiction. On the contrary, the relations of matter of fact are said to be contingent, and the denial of a factual claim is not inconceivable. Consequently, logical truths are different from factual truths in that logical truths are necessary and the factual truths are contingent.

Hume, for instance, who was a radical skeptic, did not extend his scepticism to logic. He assumed, like Husserl later, the truths of logic to be necessary, quite distinct from the truths of fact.

This belief that the realm of logic is radically distinct from matters of fact is a long-standing idea that Husserl defends against psychologism.

Husserl arrived to the conclusion that if logic is really a pure science, then logical truths should not be derived from or based on facts and experience, as psychologism contends.

Psychologism fails to distinguish between the act of judgement and the content of judgement. The act of judgement is real while the content of the judgement is ideal. The psychological act of judgement is under psychological laws, but not the content of the judgement, which is not a real part of consciousness. The ideal-logical content of a judgement is under the logical laws.

For example, psychologists interpret the absolute validity of the principle of contradiction as the factual impossibility of thinking a contradiction. Husserl points out that logical laws do not have to do with factual or real impossibility but with ideal impossibility. What is affirmed or rejected in a logical judgement is not the real psychological act of judgement but the ideal-logical content of judgement. Husserl proves this point with the following argument: The negation of a law of logic is indeed able to be performed, although such a negation would be absurd, but the negation of a psychological law cannot be performed. For example, the principle of contradiction establishes that "it is impossible that A is non-A in the same sense," but anyone can perform the negation of this principle and say that "it is possible that A is non-A," although it is a contradiction. On the contrary, a psychological law —like all natural laws— is performed without an option for its negation.[13] We can say that we are free to follow logical laws, although a rejection of one of them is a contradiction, but we are

20

not free to follow natural laws, nature, and our psychological nature, follow natural laws without the possibility of rejecting them, although natural laws (an psychological laws) sometimes fail.

In summary, logical laws are atemporal or ideally transtemporal and absolutely valid in any circumstance. The aforementioned example of the principle of noncontradiction has a universal and absolute validity, it does not depend on natural laws or any empirical law. As it was shown before, if logical laws depend on human psychological constitution, an alteration in this psychological constitution of thinking is always a possibility. It cannot be excluded absolutely, and if it occurs, the absolute validity of logical laws will be in question.

What in philosophical literature is called "eternal truth" is what Husserl called "truth-in-itself," which retains its absolute validity regardless of what happens in the real world. Truth-in-itself, like the laws of logic, are "not suspended somewhere in the void, but is rather a unity of validity in the atemporal realm of ideas." [14]

What Husserl calls "pure logic" is the formal conditions (logical conditions) of knowledge. These formal conditions or logical conditions of knowledge do not express the essence of our human thinking (what expresses this is psychology and its laws), but only that it protects us from logical or formal contradiction.

Husserl's notion of pure logic and its relations to philosophy can be summarized in the following points:

(1) Husserl has in mind two kinds of logic: the traditional logic or normative logic, and pure logic. Pure logic is in reality a theory of science, a doctrine of the formal conditions for true assertions, as was stated before.

(2) With pure logic as the formal conditions of knowledge, philosophy can regain its own domain of research without being reduced to psychology.

(3) Pure logic opens a whole range of philosophical insights into the theory of science. After separating logic from psychology, what is left is how pure logic is regulative of the concrete psychological process of thinking, how we follow the logical laws. This analysis is made in the second volume of *Logical Investigations* that contains the six investigations. (The first volume of *Logical Investigations* stresses the radical distinction between logic and psychology, and the second part goes back to the psychological processes that are correlates of the logical content.)

(4) Pure logic as the formal conditions of knowledge —in the tradition of Leibniz— is a formal *mathesis universalis*, that is to say, a universal theory of formal deductive systems.

(5) The theory of pure logic is an ideal science. This is a

21

consequence of its radical distinction from psychological laws and any other natural law. In this sense, Husserl calls the realm of logical laws ideal, or ideal being-in-itself, which is not to be confused with any form of Platonism. The notion of ideality is a realm which is required to differentiate what belongs to logic and what belongs to natural law. These differences expressed under the term "ideality" are the following:

Pure Logic	Natural Law
A priori	Empirical or a posteriori
Absolute validity	Hypothetical validity (validity under conditions)
Formal condition of knowledge	Material conditions

Once Husserl defined the characteristics of pure logic versus psychological laws, it is important to note that the rejection of logical psychologism may not be separated from a phenomenological psychology, in the way Brentano conceived this discipline.[15] As we will see in the rest of this chapter, phenomenological psychology is not genetic psychology, a psychology involved in the study of the natural laws of thinking, but a descriptive psychology, which simply and purely describes what happens in the realm of our consciousness in order to extract what is essential in it. What Husserl has in mind here is not just a descriptive psychology immersed in the particularity of our mind, but an *eidetic-descriptive psychology* which studies the essential (eidetic) characteristics of what is the act and content of consciousness.

We will see more about pure logic in Chapter 4, Section 5 in the context of the transcendental phenomenology.

4. Analysis of Intentionality

The second part of *Logical Investigations* consists of six investigations. The first deals with expression and meaning; the second is a study of meaningful species as universal objects; the third investigation deals with the theory of whole and parts, a development of Brentano's metaphysics of wholes and parts (accidents and substances); the fourth investigation is dedicated to the notion of pure grammar, a branch of pure logic that studies the laws of permissible combinations of meanings; the fifth investigation is an exhaustive clarification of Brentano's idea of intentionality; and finally, the sixth investigation is, in some way, the continuation of the first and fifth investigations and culminates with a theory of categories and a theory of truth and evidence.

Husserl always looked upon his *Logical Investigations* as the work that made the break-through to phenomenology, and the real beginning of the phenomenological movement. The main objective of the whole work was to bring out the correlation between the subjectivity of knowing (the psychological act) and the objectivity of the content of knowledge or intentional object. In this sense, Husserl's work is a development of Brentano's psychology, not only in the content but in the method, namely, the method of descriptive or phenomenological psychology.

4.1. Phenomenology of Meaning

Husserl dedicated the first logical investigation to the study of the expression and its meaning. He conceived of this investigation as a first stage in his descriptive or phenomenological psychology that would open full access to our mental life. Husserl describes what is an expression and its meaning not from the point of view of the third person, the observer, but from the point of view of the speaker, in first person. This is the more appropriate method for a descriptive psychology.

Expressions such as names and sentences are a type of sign, that is to say, something that stands for something else. What distinguishes expressions from other signs like gestures is that expressions always convey meaning.[16]

Expressions have not only meaning but a reference to an object. "Each expression not merely says something, but says something; it not only has a meaning, but refers to certain objects."[17] So, we have here two elements, meaning and the reference to an object, but an expression has a reference to an object only because it has meaning.[18] Meaning is the element through which an expression refers to an object, it does not matter if the expression is a universal name or common name, or a proper name.[19] That is to say, without meaning there is no reference (there is no rigid designation or fixed reference outside of meaning *à la* Kripke.)

Husserl stresses that *the object of reference never coincides with the meaning.* The reasons are simple, (i) two expressions can have different meanings but refer to the same object. For example, the expressions "the victor of Jena" and "the defeated of Waterloo" refer to the same object (the person of Napoleon), but they have different meanings. Furthermore, (ii) two expressions can have the same meaning but different references to an object. For example, the name "horse" has the same meaning in these two expressions, but the reference is different: "Bucefalus is a horse" and "this working animal

23

is a horse." In both expressions, "horse" has the same meaning but different reference to an object. In the first expression, "horse" refers to Bucefalus, in the second expressions, to a working animal. In reality, this happens with all universal names. The term "one" always has the same meaning, but the reference objective is different every time we use this term to refer to this object or any other object in counting.

Expressions (written or spoken) have two very different parts that form a sort of unity: a physical part made of sounds or traces on a paper, and an ideal part, which is the meaning. The physical part of an expression has all the characteristics of a physical reality (three dimensions, temporality, etc.). On the contrary, the ideal part —the meaning— of an expression does not share any of these characteristics of a physical thing at all. Meanings are not tridimensional and they are not temporal. The meaning of the term "horse" persists when the physical part (the impressed letters) of "horse" disappears, even if there are no horses any more. Expressions are physical things animated by non physical things (the meaning.) Nevertheless, the physical part of an expression does not contribute at all to the meaning of the expression, in other words, the essence of an expression is only its meaning.[20] Husserl goes as far as to say that in some cases the physical part of an expression can disappear completely.[21] The physical part of an expression is just mere support for the meaning; it can cease to be the support of the meaning and become a simple physical object, and as a consequence it ceases to be an expression. It can be substituted by any physical object as support of a meaning. (We can decide that the meaning horse is expressed by the term "esroh"). In other words, the physical part of an expression is completely indifferent to what it means. This does not mean that now Husserl does not recognize the unity of an expression: the two parts of an expression —physical and ideal— have a particular unity, the meaning and the physical part of an expression are put together (they are united or fused) by means of our consciousness. This unity is very particular because both parts are not only completely different, but also they are mutually independent; nevertheless they are able to form a unity by means of some consciousness.

Why does Husserl think that the meaning is ideal? Here are some reasons:

(1) We can reiterate the same expression to express the same meaning. But in reality there is not the same expression. While we can repeat the same physical pattern of an expression, properly speaking, there are not equal meanings. What we call equal meaning is in reality identical meaning. For example, the number 3 said by me is not equal to the number 3 said by you, they are exactly identical,

otherwise we should admit that there are different numbers 3. Husserl finds the same situation with meanings: *the meaning is just identical in the repetition of expressions with the same pattern.* "What a statement means is always the same, regardless of whom is affirming the statement, and regardless of the circumstances and time in which it is affirmed."[22] This identity of meaning with a plurality of expressions (the term "horse" uttered now and before, by me and by you are different physical objects, but the meaning is identical) is called by Husserl ideality. Therefore, *the meaning is the ideal identity of a multiplicity of expressions.*

(2) While the physical part of an expression is subject to time, the meaning is timeless. When I pronounce a sentence, the meaning does not appear in that point of time like the words, but the meaning reappears to me as identical. When I utter the word "horse," it is created for a period of time, but the meaning is not created like a term. I bring to consciousness the meaning, while the words are being created. While the words are ephemeral the meaning is always there, atemporal. The meaning of the mathematical expression "$a^2+b^2=c^2$ is true regardless of the fact of whether or not Pythagoras discovered it, and regardless whether or not it is pronounced by anyone. In this sense, the meaning is said to be ideal. Meaning does not have time as its form of being, so there is not properly production of meaning but production of the physical part of the expression.

What produces the unity between meaning and the physical part of an expression is a mental act, what Husserl calls "the meaning-conferring act," which also is called meaning-intention (*Bedeutungsintention*). The meaning-conferring act is an intentional act (see next section) that has the function of bringing the meaning to the sign to form the unity of the expression.[23] The relation between meaning and the corresponding meaning-conferring act has something in common with the relation between the physical part of an expression and its meaning: the meaning is atemporal, ideal; on the contrary, the meaning-conferring act is ephemeral, a real part of consciousness subject to time.

Husserl distinguishes between the meaning-conferring act (the meaning-intention) and the meaning-fulfilling act. The latter has as its intentional object those objects or instances that are cases or examples of the meaning. For example, the word "table" has the meaning of table given in a meaning-conferring act. When I perceive an individual table, existing in a moment of time, or I imagine one, this individual is the intentional object of a meaning-fulfilling act, an object that fulfills the meaning, but is not part of the meaning and it is not even the essence of an expression.[24]

25

We can summarize this analysis in the following way:

	Objective Pole	Subjective Pole
	Meaning (ideal part of the expression)	Meaning-conferring act
Elements of Expression	Written or spoken signs (physical part of the expression)	˙
	Object (the referent)	
	Object of fulfillment (perceived or imagined)	Meaning-fulfilling act

The object-referent of the meaning-conferring act is identical to the object-referent of the meaning-fulfilling act, but the object of fulfillment is not the object-referent. If the meaning-fulfilling act is an act of external perception, the object-referent is not perceived adequately but by sides. The perception of the morning star is not the same as the whole object-referent Venus.

One of the most bizarre philosophical analyses of Husserl's phenomenology is the relation between meaning and universal. Both meaning and universal are species in Husserl's terminology. A species is characterized by both being ideal and being able to have individuals. For example, the universal "horse" is a species. It is ideal like meaning because the universal horse does not exist, what exists is this and that horse. We perceive individual horses not the horse (the universal horse). The universal horse has many individuals (the extension of the universal horse) that have real existence. Now, the problem comes when Husserl asks for the individuals of the meaning. We know that the meaning is given in the meaning-conferring act or meaning-intention. Any time we say a word, a meaning-conferring act appears in a point of time, and the meaning reappears as the intentional object of the meaning-conferring act. Husserl establishes that the individuals of the meaning will have to be the meaning-conferring acts, as the individuals of the universal horse are the individual horses. This means that a proposition just as the meaning of an expression has the individual acts of judgement as its individuals. In other words, meaning and universals are different categories. Universals belong to the physical region while meanings don't because they belong to the psychical category (?). I think that Husserl here was not as penetrating and insightful as in the rest of his work. To clarify this issue, consider the following points. (i) The universal of individual mental acts is the

26

universal mental act; so, the universal of a concrete and individual meaning-conferring act is the universal meaning-conferring act and not the meaning. (ii) Husserl thought that because identical meaning is brought to our consciousness by certain mental acts or meaning-conferring acts, and not by others, he drew the conclusion that they were the individuals of the meaning. But we could say the same thing in relation to other mental acts and their corresponding intentional objects. For example, blue is the intentional object of certain acts of perception and no others; therefore, the intentional object blue is the species of these acts of perception. Something that is clearly erroneous.[25]

Husserl dropped this misleading idea in the second edition of *Logical Investigations* (1911), but some shadows of the idea remains. For example, in the second edition of 1911 Husserl says that the identity of meaning is the identity of the species (the species is identical in all the individuals), an ideal unity that embraces the individual meaning-conferring acts.[26]

Universals are another kind of species, ideal in character. The individuals of universals are the temporal individuals, but the universal as such is atemporal in a similar manner as meanings. Universals are the intentional objects of a specific mode of consciousness that cannot be reduced to the modes in which individuals are apprehended.[27] This idea goes against the empiricism of Locke.

* * *

After these analyses of expressions and universals, Husserl develops a mereology, that is to say, a formal ontology, which studies the formal-logical conditions under which a material ontology (classical ontology, the science of real beings) is possible. This formal ontology is important to understand some terminology of the following analysis of the acts of consciousness, including the meaning-conferring acts.

In the third investigation of *Logical Investigations*, Husserl starts from Brentano's ideas of whole and part, objects that are dependent and objects that are independent. For example, the physical part of an expression is an independent object, there is nothing in the nature of the physical voice that implies a meaning. But as we will see later, different parts of a mental act can be dependent objects, that is to say, they necessitate each other.

4.2. Analysis of the Intentional Act

Probably, the most interesting analysis of Husserl's *Logical Investigations* is the analysis of intentionality, which is mainly a development in depth of Brentano's notion of intentionality, but with

27

important influence from the theory of objects of Alexius Meinong, who was another disciple of Brentano at the same time as Husserl.

Husserl begins with a delimitation of the notion of consciousness to intentional experiences or, in Husserl's parlance, *acts*.

The starting point, which is an evident axiom for phenomenology, is that it is a fact of inner perception that mental acts have the essential characteristic of intentionality. It is not possible to think without thinking of something (an object); it is not possible to see without seeing something (a color), and so on. The characteristic of these mental acts (thinking, seeing, etc.) of referring to something else is called "intentionality." Husserl, in this stage distinguishes between the object that is intentionally targeted (the real object) and the object precisely as it is intended (the intentional object). In reality, this distinction is only provisional because, from the point of view of our subjectivity (which is the point of view of phenomenology), *every object is an intentional object.*

As we mentioned above, the method Husserl uses is in the line of Brentano's descriptive psychology, which consists of a description of the activity of consciousness in its essential or eidetic structure. And like Brentano, Husserl seeks for a phenomenological science of consciousness without presuppositions but without still questioning the realism of extramental objects. In order to accomplish this, phenomenology restricts itself only to evident data. In the parlance of *Logical Investigations*, evident data are only adequate data, self-given data. The realm of adequate data is the immanent content of consciousness given in phenomenological reflection. The external world is not a self-given datum, only the immanent content of consciousness in whose stream we live is the closest datum we have. Husserl agrees with Brentano that we are absolutely certain about having a thought or a visual experience, but we do not have absolute certainty about a physical event (maybe our senses deceive us, or our senses are not as accurate as we assume.)

The content of consciousness is double: (i) the actual (*reell*) immanent content of consciousness, with the counterpole (ii) the actual (*real*) and ideal objects. These are called "moments" of consciousness in Husserl's terminology. An important difference from Brentano, but similar to Kant, Husserl considers that actually immanent contents of consciousness do not need to be only intentional acts, they can be nonintentional such as immanent data of sensation.

Husserl distinguishes several kinds of intentional acts according to their eidetic structure (or essential structure). The eidetic structure of an intentional act derives from the phenomenological description of these acts. In the description of an intentional act we can see that it has

28

the essential property of intentionality, by which an intentional act has an intentional object. In this sense, one can say that the object of an intentional act is an intentional object, that is to say, that there is an act with a determinately characterized intention, "an intention that in this determinateness makes up precisely what we call the intention toward this object."[28]   Now, thus characterized the object as an intentional object (notice that here "intentional object" is not what commonly is called "object," which is identified with thing), "there are ... not two things present in immanent experience: the object, which would not be immanently experienced and then next to it the intentional, immanent experience itself [the intentional act] ... rather, only one thing is present, the intentional, immanent experience, of which the essential descriptive characteristic is precisely the relevant intention."[29]   When we experience our intentional act, there is not an immanent experience of this act, and separatedly, an external experience of its object.   If we take into consideration that we are talking about intentional objects (the intention of an intentional act), then in the same experience by which we immanently experience the intentional act we experience its intentional object.   We do not need two experiences, one for the act and another for the intentional object.

The different kinds of intentional acts will correspond to the different kinds of intentional objects or intentions.   Thus, Husserl distinguishes acts of judgement, acts of memory, and so on, inasmuch as there are different intentional objects (a proposition, a memory, etc.).

One of the main theses of Brentano's philosophy is that any mental act either is a presentation or is based on a presentation.   For example, the color red is a phenomenon of a presentation, but the proposition "this table is red" is apprehended by a judgement that is first based on the presentation of red.   Husserl partially accepts this important Brentanian thesis.   For Husserl, *the characteristic of presenting an objectivity is common to all intentional acts regardless of their type* (judgement, emotion, etc.).   The various types of intentional acts all belong to the same class of objectifying acts.[30]   So, while for Brentano, presentation is a sort of mental act different from others such as judgement and emotion,[31] for Husserl presentation is a characteristic of all intentional acts. Any intentional act has the eidetic property of an intention to an objectivity, which is the same as saying that any intentional act objectifies something, that is to say, they are objectifying acts.   The presentation of an act is its property of intentionality.   (We will see later here what makes all intentional acts a presentation is the moment[32] matter of an act.)   From these analyses, we see that objectifying acts are other expressions for intentional acts, both present an object to consciousness or, in other words, both refer to

29

an intentional object, or both make that something plays the role of an object for consciousness. All these expressions are equivalent.

Husserl distinguishes between the object to which an act in its totality is directed and the objects to which the partial acts (which are parts of the total act), are directed. For example, the act of judgement that we produce when we say that "the pencil is on the table" implies the object of the whole act of judgement (the proposition the pencil is on the table) and the objects of the partial acts that are part of the total act (the presentations of pencil, table, and the relations between both).

One of the most impressive achievements of the phenomenology of *Logical Investigations* is the distinction between the quality of act and the matter as two moments of the whole of an intentional or objectifying act. Husserl uses the phenomenological method of variation: one can vary from an experience of judging to another experience of representing while what is judging and representing is the same objectivity, and we can vary from an objectivity to another while keeping the same type of experience (representing, judging, etc.) Husserl calls "quality of act" the variation of experiences as representing, judging, etc., and he calls "matter" (*Materie*) that moment of the intentional act that varies when one varies the objectivity keeping the same type of experience (representing, judging, etc.). The quality of act is the mode in which a determined intentional object is intended. An intentional object can be intended in the mode of representing, or in the mode of judging, or in the mode of desiring, etc. The quality of act is responsible for the different kinds of intentional experiences.[33] The matter is the moment of the intentional act that has the function of presenting a determinate intentional object. "Matter was classed as that moment in an objectifying act which makes the act present just this object."[34] The matter makes the intentional act refer to a tree, a table or any other determinate object, while the quality of act makes the intentional act refer to these intentional objects in the mode of representing or judging, imagining, etc.

Husserl calls "the intentional essence" of an act the unity of matter and quality of act. Thus, we can summarize this analysis in the following formula:

The intentional essence of an act has at least two real moments, (i) the quality of act by which an intentional act objectifies something in different subjective attitudes (doubting, judging, imagining, and so on) and (ii) the matter, by which the intentional act has the intentional reference to a determinate intentional object.

The matter of an act is responsible for the presentational character of an act. Whoever is familiar with Brentano will remember that the act of presentation was the base of the rest of mental acts (something judged has to be presented before being judged). For Husserl, all acts enjoy the character of being presentations because they all have the moment matter, which makes the act be directed to a determinate object (Brentano —Husserl thinks— did not distinguish between matter and quality of act.)

Husserl says that "The matter firmly determines not only the object as such, which is meant by the act, but also the way in which it is determined."[35] This means that the matter determines both (i) denotation, namely, which object the intentional act will refer to and (ii) connotation, namely, the characteristics of this object. It also is called the *Sinn* of the act (later, it will be called the "noema" of the act).

The most elemental way of relating to a determinate object is by means of names. Here, the intentional act refers directly to the object, namely, by pointing to it. Husserl uses the expression "as if with the finger" to mean the simple way of reference to a name. The phenomenological analysis of the matter of a name yields the conclusion that this matter is "single-membered matter." The intentional act of a name means or intends the object in one ray of meaning or intention (*Meinung*).[36] On the contrary, propositional acts (also known as synthetic acts in Husserl's terminology) are multi-rayed acts (complex acts). There are many other multi-rayed acts such as collecting, relating, calculating, etc. And in general, all acts called "categorial acts" are multi-rayed acts, as we will see later. All multi-rayed acts are founded ultimately on single-rayed acts. This foundation comes from the matter. Multi-rayed matter presupposes single-rayed matter in which the members of the propositional intention are simply intended.[37] For example, "the flower is red" is a multi-rayed matter founded in simple presentations whose matters refer to the pencil and red.

The quality of act may be simple or founded as well, but there is no parallelism with the matter. Intentional acts of simple quality of act are all objectifying acts, *i.e.*, presentations, judgements, doubts, questions, etc. Nevertheless, *a founded quality of act is not an objectifying act* (an intentional act). For example, an experience of joy. This is an important departure from Brentano, for whom, all psychical phenomena are intentional acts. According to Husserl, although his master Brentano would strongly disagree, acts like the experience of joy are not direct objectifying acts. This is due to the fact that these experiences are merely subjective attitudes (they are not intentional, they are merely moods), but they presuppose an intentional relation to the object, a presentation of the object to the experience of joy. The act of joy is founded on a simple act, which is an objectifying act (a

31

presentation, a judgement). The act of joy colors the objectifying experience, but the act of joy as such does not portray an intentional relation by itself. Its intentionality is borrowed from an objectifying act.[38]

Any founded quality of act presupposes a simple quality of act, which is always an objectifying act. This objectifying act, in turns, is an act with a determinate structure in its matter, namely, a single-membered matter or a multi-membered matter. If the act of joy were founded on an objectifying act with a single-membered matter, we would have the joy of an object presented in a single ray (the joy of a blue sky, for example); if the act of joy were founded on an objectifying act with a multi-membered matter, we would have the joy of a complex and articulated object presented in a judgement (a synthetic act) or categorical act (the joy that the music is being performed, for example).

In summary, quality and matter are mutually requisite moments of the intentional act. "The quality determines only whether what has already been 'presented' [...] in a determinate way is intentionally present [...] as desirable, questionable, ..."[39] Notice that Husserl prefers to use the term "matter" instead of "content" here. The reason is simply clarity of terminology. The expression "content of an intentional act" can refer to two different things: the intentional content (the intentional object of an act) or the material content, what Husserl prefers to call "matter," which is a structural moment of any intentional act.

In this stage of Husserl's phenomenology, there is an unquestioned phenomenological realism, which is suitable for the phenomenological method as a phenomenological psychology à la Brentano. In this sense, we have the following characteristics in the analysis of an intentional act. Intentional acts are real; the quality and matter are real parts, but the content as intentional content or intentional object is not a real part of the experience. Because of this, Husserl preferred to use the term "matter" instead of the confused term "content."

4.3. Phenomenalism, Intentional Object and Representationalism

Husserl rejects three classical views in the theory of knowledge: phenomenalism, the distinction between real object and intentional object, and representationalism.

(1) Phenomenalism, as the doctrine maintained by Hume, does not distinguish between the mental act and the intentional object. For

Hume, there is no distinction between the impression of blue and the color blue, between the idea of blue and the color blue. The most fundamental axiom of Husserl's phenomenology is the intentional character of consciousness. This means that there is a distinction between mental act —a real part of consciousness— and the object, which is not a real part of consciousness, even if the object is real. While the act of consciousness is always real, the object of this act can be real or unreal. For example, the table in front of me is an intentional object of an act of consciousness. The table is not a psychological part of consciousness, it is always transcendent to it. Even if the table turned out to be an hallucination (so, it did not exist), the intentional object of my act of consciousness is still transcendent to the act of consciousness, that is to say, it is not a real part of it. It is absurd that the act of consciousness has to be blue because the intentional object is blue, or that the act of consciousness is five inches long because the intentional object is five inches long. In summary, the intentional object is nothing in the act of consciousness, it is transcendent to consciousness.

(2) Husserl explicitly states that "the intentional object of a presentation is the same as the real object, even if this is extramental, and it is an absurd to distinguish between both." [40] Obviously, the real object or the extramental object would not be the object of any act of consciousness if this object were not the intentional object. Husserl considers this statement purely and simply analytical. Any object has to be an intentional object to be an object for my consciousness.

(3) Representationalism is the doctrine that maintains that the object is represented in consciousness by means of an image. The image in consciousness would be responsible for the intentional direction toward an object. Husserl rejects this doctrine as absurd. (i) All images require physical support. How is it possible to have a physical image of something that is not physical such as a universal, a number, an abstract, etc. (ii) All images are images because they suppose the intentionality of consciousness. There is nothing in physical things that makes them images of anything; there is no internal character of physical things that makes them be images of something. Images are like expressions, they need an act of intentionality in order to be images or expressions. [41] One should not confuse an image with a likeness. Something can be a likeness of something else, but this is different from being an image. A picture, for example, is only an image for a spectator, for an observer. So, an image does not give any intentionality, but any image requires and necessitates that intentionality is established before hand.

33

4.4. The Notion of Truth and Categorial Intuition

There are two notions we have to deal with in this section. First, the notion of truth and its relation to evidence, and second, the important notion of categorial intuition. Both ideas are contained in the sixth investigation of Husserl's *Logical Investigations*, and are closely related. Truth belongs to judgements, and, according to Husserl, a judgement is a categorial act.

Husserl's doctrine of truth is based on the notion of intuitive fulfillment. As we saw above (Section 5.1. "Phenomenology of Meaning"), a meaning-fulfillment act can fulfill an empty meaning, for example, the meaning bird may be fulfilled with the perception of this bird in my visual field. A meaning-fulfillment act is an intuition of the object "in person," the object is given directly. It is said that the meaning was empty, and it is fulfilled by an intuitive act. We can enhance slightly this notion and say that a fulfillment is a cognitive act by which an empty intention is connected synthetically with the corresponding intuition.[42] The synthesis between the empty intention and the corresponding intuition can be confirmed in diverse degrees until the extreme of being disappointed. That is to say, there are degrees of fulfillment from the perfect confirmation to deception, disagreement, and discrepancy.[43] The experience of fulfillment is the experience of a complex interconnection of different forms of intentional acts. The phenomenological analysis of this experience yields the following result: (i) the intentional act that has to be fulfilled, which is empty or partially empty (a meaning-intention); (ii) the fulfilling act itself, an intuition of the object "in persona," and (iii) the experience of the synthesis.

It is important to notice that both the intentional act that has to be fulfilled and the fulfilling act refer to the same object, but in different ways.[44] The former refers to the object but it does not present the object "in person." The latter refers to the object by presenting it "in person;" it brings the object to intuitive givenesss. If both intentional acts did not refer to the same object, fulfillment would not be possible. The process of fulfillment brings two intentional acts into synthetic relation: it is a synthetic relation between their intentional objects. Now, which intentional act plays the role of a fulfilling act? Is perception the adequate act to fulfill an empty intention, a meaning, for example?

Here is an example given by Husserl that explains this problem. The judgement "the black bird flies off" is an empty intention (an empty assertion), which can be fulfilled in a synthetic relation with an act of perception of the bird in question (the bird's being black.)

Husserl rightly notices that a sense perception cannot fulfill a *predicative* assertion; in the best of cases —like in the example— the fulfilling is very limited. The perception of a black bird is not enough to fulfill the predicative assertion "the black bird flies off." Perception is always of an object given in a certain perspective, we perceive only one side of the object. From one perspective one perceives one side, from another perspective another side. But these accidental sides of the object perceived should be reflected in the assertion. There should be as many assertions as possible sides of the object given by perception. In other words, based on the same perception of the bird, the assertion could be very different and manifest a very different meaning. Based on the perception of this bird, I could have said the assertion "this is black," or "this is a black bird," or "this black bird flies off," and so on. And vice versa, the assertion could be the same, while the perception changes in many ways. Perception depends on the relative position of the person who perceives. Different persons who perceive the same object never have exactly the same perception; they perceive different sides. In conclusion, the meaning of an assertion seems to be unaltered by the various differences in the singular and personal perceptions, and this meaning is something common to all these acts of perceptions corresponding to a single object.[45]

We need something more than sheer perception. Here Husserl introduces the notion of categorial intuition. An empty intention like a predicative assertion, is fulfilled in a categorial intention, and through this, the empty intention reaches its reference to the perceptual object. What fulfilled the empty predicative assertion is a categorial intuition and not a sense intuition, and through the categorial intuition, the empty intention can refer to the object of the perception.

Meaning-conferring acts gain cognitional relevance only when they are fulfilled by the appropriate categorial intuition. When this fulfillment takes place, the referent of a meaning-conferring act is no longer an empty intention but self-given in intuition.

A categorial act is a judgement. So, we have two sorts of categorial acts, empty intentions such as meanings (categorial semantic intentions), and categorial intuitions. This distinction is based on the characteristic of the intentional object. If the object is intuitively given, we have a categorial intuition. If the object is given by a sign, we have an empty or signitive categorial act. Before saying more about categorial intuition, we have to analyze a little more the notion of categorial acts in general.

Categorial acts are of a different variety. Acts of conjoining, distinguishing, relating, counting, etc. are categorial acts, which are intentional acts with a complex matter. The intentional object of a

35

categorial act is neither a sense object nor a physical one, just as the categorial act is neither a sense act nor a physical act. Husserl calls the object of a categorial act ideal object, which is a higher order object.

Categorial acts are synthetic acts in which some pre-given stuff acquires a logical form. This logico-formational activity is neither an absolute spontaneous activity of thinking nor a completely independent one. Any categorial act presupposes necessarily the pre-given stuff that has to be structured in a logical form. This pre-given stuff is ultimately sense stuff: "everything categorial ultimately rests upon sense intuitions"[46] and without a sense foundation, there is no thinking at all. A priori judgements are based on sense experience as well. For example, the assertion "red is different than yellow" is a priori, but it presupposes the pre-given sense stuff of red and yellow.

The characteristic of an intuition is to be able to present the object directly (in person); the object is immediately given. The intentional object of an intuition can be both a sense object (this color red) or a categorial object (the idea of horse). Sense objects are objects of inferior order; while ideal objects are of higher order.[47] For example, "a dove is now sitting on my window sill." The meaning is a proposition, an ideal object such as a number. In the above proposition, dove and window are real objects, but the whole proposition is an ideal object, something that one does not expect to find among the objects of the world.[48] Intuitions of sense objects are perceptions (external perceptions), intuitions of categorial objects are categorial intuitions or intellectual intuitions. The novelty of Husserl is to describe the fact that we have intellectual intuitions, intuitions of categories as we have intuitions of sense objects.

The intentional object of acts of categorial intuition are *self-given*. It seems to be clear that Husserl extrapolates the self-given model of a sense object to a categorial object. (Perhaps Husserl is not completely free of an intuitionism naively oriented toward the process of seeing, at least in his *Logical Investigations*.) How is a self-giveness of a categorial object possible? Kant admitted only the self-giveness of sense experience and rejected strongly any intellectual intuition. Husserl, on the contrary, admits sense and intellectual intuitions. But how the latter is possible, is better answered later in *Ideas*: the intuitional giveness of categorial objects is a result of the doctrine of eidetic variation we will see in the next chapter. It is very important not to conceive of the categorial intuition as the *intuitu originarius*, that is to say, a privileged intuition of objects regardless of experience. The categorial intuition is an authentic act of thought based on sense experience.[49] The domain of empty categorial acts (meaning-intentions) is much wider that of the categorial intuition. There are infinite empty meanings which cannot find the corresponding categorial intuition that fulfills them. In the final analysis, *categorial intuition is the mode in which other categorial objectivities such as states of affairs (that S is P) are intuitively given.*

From the point of view of epistemology, we have to distinguish among intentional acts, those which are acts of knowledge, and those which are not. An act of knowledge is, as in Kant, an act of scientific knowledge versus other acts that do not constitute scientific knowledge. Only some intentional acts constitute knowledge in the strict sense. Neither the empty meaning-intention nor the categorial intuition are acts of knowledge in the strict sense. A categorial intuition becomes knowledge in the strict sense when there is a synthetic agreement with an empty intention. Kant and Husserl agree that pure and mere intuitions are epistemologically blind if they are not subsumed under meaning-intention, and pure and mere meaning-intentions are empty if they do not have intuitional confirmation. The difference between Kant and Husserl here is in the extension of the notion of intuition, which in Kant is restricted only to sense intuition, and in Husserl is extended to intellectual intuition or categorial intuition. The consciousness of the fulfillment of an empty intention with a categorial intuition is called recognition of the intentional object in the concept.[50]

Now we have all the elements to describe the phenomenon of truth and evidence. Husserl describes the phenomenon of evidence as *the experience of truth.* And truth is the adequacy of the judgement to the thing itself.[51]   (For Husserl, what is objectively given in the intuition is what it is.)   This adequacy is not understood in the classical sense but as the *agreement between what is meant and what is given as such*,[52] which is a consummation of the synthesis of fulfillment we were analyzing above. Because there are degrees of fulfillment, degrees of synthesis between an intuition and an empty intention, then there will be degrees of experiences of this synthesis, that is to say, *degrees of evidence.* All these analyses are an important departure from both the classical theory of truth as correspondence and the notion of evidence.

Truth is the objective correlate of the synthesis of fulfillment: the intentional objects of both acts agree or adequate each other. Evidence is the experience of this agreement, or as Husserl puts it, the immanent experience of truth. Notice that truth is defined from the point of view of the intentional object, while evidence is defined from the point of view of the experience or intentional act. This does not mean that evidence is a subjective characteristic of experience, but a specific experience of an objective situation of agreement. Evidence is the consciousness of an objective agreement.

Because all categorial acts presuppose pre-given sense stuff, sense intuitions will be the ultimate foundation of truth (through the categorial intuition).

To appreciate the differences between the classical theory of truth and evidence and the Husserlian approach, let us consider some points of comparison. Aquinas, for example, defines truth as the *adaequatio intellectus et rei* (the adequacy of the intellect and the thing). If we take Aquinas's definition of truth as the classical one, we will notice essential differences between this philosopher and Husserl.

(1) There is no single text in Aquinas in which truth is defined as the adequacy of the intellect and the *object*. Aquinas uses the term "thing" and not "object" to define the truth. For him, a thing is an entity in the world, and an object is an external reference of the thing to the thinker. If truth has to be defined with the notion of object instead of thing, then, Aquinas thinks, all our statements would be true.

(2) Husserl describes truth as synthetical agreement between two intentional objects.

(3) For Aquinas, evidence does not have degrees.

(4) For Husserl evidence has degrees matching the degrees of fulfillment.

* * *

With the phenomenological analysis of truth, Husserl achieves his goal in *Logical Investigations* of developing the correlation between the subjectivity of knowing and the objectivity of the intentional content of knowledge. He accomplished this, first, by attacking the psychologist version of logic, second, by defining the domain of pure logic, third, by describing the phenomenon of meaning, fourth, by analyzing the Brentanian notion of intentionality, and finally, by describing the notion of categorial intuition, truth and evidence. In all these subjects, Husserl established the radical separation between the intentional object and the intentional act, between the objective content of knowledge and the mental process, or in a nutshell, an analysis of the two poles of consciousness. In all these analyses, Husserl used the phenomenological method as a descriptive psychology. It is only later, that Husserl will study directly the method he used in *Logical Investigations*.

ENDNOTES

[1] Cf. Edmund Husserl, *Philosophie der Arithmetik*, in *Husserliana* XII, 1970, pp.287ff.

[2] Cf. G. Frege, "Review of Husserl's *Philosophie der Arithmetik*", translation by E.W. Kluge, in *Mind*, LXXXI (1972): 321-37.

[3] Cf. Edmund Husserl, *Logical Investigations*, volume I, translated by J. N. Findlay, London, Routledge & Kegan Paul, 1970, § 19.

[4] This is taken from Husserl, *Logical Investigations*, vol. I, Chapters 4 and 7.

[5] Cf. Husserl *Logical Investigations*, vol. I, § 16

[6] Cf. Husserl, *Logical Investigations*, vol. I, § 40.

[7] Cf. Husserl, *Logical Investigations*, vol. I, § 22.

[8] Husserl, *Logical Investigations*, vol. I, § 19.

[9] Cf. Husserl, *Logical Investigations*, vol. I, §§ 39, 40.

[10] Husserl, *Logical Investigations*, vol. I, § 30.

[11] Husserl, *Logical Investigations*, vol. I, § 31.

[12] Husserl, *Logical Investigations*, vol. I, § 31.

[13] Cf. Husserl, *Logical Investigations*, vol. I, § 39.

[14] Husserl, *Logical Investigations*, vol. I, § 38.

[15] Cf. Franz Brentano, *Descriptive Psychology*, transl. by Benito Müller, London and New York, Routledge, 1982.

[16] Cf. Husserl, *Logical Investigations*, vol. II, Inv. I, § 1.

[17] Husserl, *Logical Investigations*, vol. II, Inv. I, § 12.

[18] Cf. Husserl, *Logical Investigations*, vol. II, Inv. I, § 13.

[19] Cf. Husserl, *Logical Investigations*, vol. II, Inv. VI, § 7.

[20] Cf. Husserl, *Logical Investigations*, vol. II, Inv. I, § 13.

[21] Cf. Husserl, *Logical Investigations*, vol. II, Inv. V, § 19.

[22] Husserl, *Logical Investigations*, vol. II, Inv. I, § 11.

[23] Cf. Husserl, *Logical Investigations*, vol. II, Inv. I, § 18.

[24] Husserl, *Logical Investigations*, vol. II, Inv. I, § 9.

[25] Husserl conceives of universals as objects, but not meaning. The idea of meaning seems to resist being called an object. But as Meinong proved in his theory of objects, it is perfectly feasible to conceive of meanings as objects if one understands object as the terminus of an intentional act.

[26] Cf. Husserl, *Logical Investigations*, vol. II, § 31.

[27] Cf. Husserl, *Logical Investigations*, vol. II, Inv. II, § 1.

[28] Husserl, *Logical Investigation*, vol. II, Inv. V, § 20.

[29] Husserl,, *Logical Investigations*, vol. II, Inv. V, §11a.

[30] Cf. Husserl, *Logical Investigations*, vol. II, Inv. V, §41.

[31] Brentano distinguishes at least three classes of mental acts: presentations, judgements, and phenomena of love and hate.

[32] Moment in Husserl 's formal ontology is a part of a whole.

[33] Cf. Husserl, *Logical Investigations*, vol. II, Inv. V, § 20.

[34] Husserl, *Logical Investigations*, vol. II, Inv. VI, § 25.

[35] Husserl, *Logical Investigations*, vol. II, Inv. V, § 20.

[36] Cf. Husserl, *Logical Investigations*, vol. II, Inv. V, § 33.

[37] Cf. Husserl, *Logical Investigations*, vol. II, Inv. V, § 42.

[38] Cf. Husserl, *Logical Investigations*, vol. II, Inv. V, §§ 37 41.

[39] Husserl, *"Logical Investigations*, vol. II, Inv. V, § 20.

[40] Cf. Husserl, *Logical Investigations*, vol. II, Inv. V, Appendix to §§ 11 and 20.

[41] Cf. Husserl, *Logical Investigations*, vol. II, Inv. V, Appendix to §§ 11 and 20.

[42] Cf. Husserl, *Logical Investigations*, vol. II, Inv. VI, § 8.

[43] Cf. Husserl, *Logical Investigations*, vol. II, Inv. VI, § 11.

[44] Cf. Husserl, *Logical Investigations*, vol. II, Inv. VI, § 28.

[45] Cf. Husserl, *Logical Investigations*, II, Inv. VI, § 4.

[46] Husserl, *Logical Investigations*, vol. II, Inv. VI, § 60.

[47] Cf. Husserl, *Logical Investigations*, vol. II, Inv. VI, § 46.

[48] Cf. Husserl, *Logical Investigations*, vol. II, Inv. VI, § 60.

[49] Cf. Husserl, *Logical Investigations*, vol. II, Inv. VI, § 24.

[50] Cf. Husserl, *Logical Investigations*, II, Inv. VI, § 8.

[51] Cf. Husserl, *Logical Investigations*, vol. II, Inv. VI, § 37.

[52] Cf. Husserl, *Logical Investigations*, vol. II, Inv. VI, § 39.

3

The Phenomenological Method

1. Radicality of Phenomenology: Freedom of Presuppositions

In *Logical Investigations*, Husserl partially applied the phenomenological method as a phenomenological psychology borrowed from Brentano, without explicitly making the very method a subject of study. In Husserl's main work —*Ideas Pertaining to a Pure Phenomenology and to a Phenomenological Philosophy, First Book: General Introduction to Pure Phenomenology* (1913)— Husserl exposes the phenomenological method in depth. Husserl's plan was to write a synthesis of phenomenology as a rigorous science, with the first book dedicated to the phenomenological method, the second book to the relations among phenomenology and the rest of the sciences (physics, psychology, etc.), and the third book to the place of phenomenology in philosophy and its relation with metaphysics. Here, we will examine Husserl's proposal for the method of phenomenology and its status as a science.

Husserl is looking for a philosophy which is the most radical possible, that is to say, presuppositionless. This is the Cartesian ideal of philosophy that Husserl accepts in spirit but not in the letter. Husserl expresses this ideal in the following way: "In making its first appearance, phenomenology must reckon with a fundamental mood of skepticism. It demands the most perfect freedom from presuppositions and, concerning itself, an absolute reflective insight."[1] There are two elements here to achieve a presuppositionless science: (i) absolute intellectual *evidence* and (ii) the general procedure of phenomenology, namely, the *reflection of itself.*

Husserl's passion for clarity and certainty led him from mathematics to logic, from logic to philosophy, and from philosophy

41

in general to phenomenology as a special kind of seeing that could be cultivated by training and practice, as we will see in this chapter.

Although Husserl follows the Cartesian ideal, he considers Descartes to have been inconsistent with this ideal. Husserl proposes to start again from consciousness and its contents, that is to say, the experiences of the ego. Freedom from presuppositions is for Husserl the condition of all philosophy, and it means (i) not to take authority as a presupposition, (ii) not to take cultural tradition, scientific tradition, and scientific theories as presuppositions, that is to say, freedom of theories, including metaphysics, and, as an important consequence, (iii) not to take the results of positive science as a presupposition.

The last point deserves some comment. Positive sciences, such as physics, take for granted the existence of the object of study. They take for granted the causal relation among facts. Furthermore, positive science is based on empirical knowledge, which does not have absolute certainty. Empirical knowledge is only a probabilistic knowledge that can be refuted later with other empirical knowledge, and, in turn, this empirical knowledge can be refuted with new empirical evidence. Husserl is looking for a starting point that does not presuppose this uncertainty, and he believes he has found it in our conscious life, the description of what is given in intuition. So, phenomenology is restricted to the description of the insight or intuition of what is given in our internal experience. To describe what is given or has appeared to me does not need any presupposition of positive science, nor even metaphysics. Both—metaphysics and positive science—deal with facts, casual relations, etc. which are subject to the uncertainty of experience. Phenomenology contains no statement on existence, it is purely and simply a description of how things are given or appear to our consciousness; so, no presupposition from metaphysics, physics, psychology, etc. can be the starting point of phenomenology. In this sense, phenomenology is a presuppositionless science.

The only source of knowledge for phenomenology is the evidence of immanent data. Phenomenology is a method of access to consciousness in order to analyze it. As we saw in the second chapter, one of the most evident data of consciousness is the essential characteristic of intentionality, by which mental acts refer to an object (an intentional object). So, the field of consciousness implies mental acts and the intentional objects of these acts. When an act refers intentionally to an object, the ego is present in the intentional act. For example, when I think of a horse, the terminus horse is the intentional object; thinking is the mental act, and I, the ego, is present in the exercise of the mental act. Given this analysis, we have the following structure: *I—think—something*. This is the main structure that phenomenology studies. Husserl expresses this structure of consciousness in his own terminology: *Ego—cogito—cogitatum*. Everything we know is a *cogitatum* (what is thought), which is the intentional object in the terminology of *Logical Investigations*. The mental act is the *cogito* (the act of thinking), and the ego accompanies the mental act in referring to the intentional object. Phenomenology is then a study or reflection on this structure (*ego cogito cogitatum*). We will say more about this later.

Given the freedom of presuppositions, phenomenological analysis does not depend on language, nor the existence of the world, nor even the existence of human beings. Maybe everything is a fiction, but even in this case, phenomenological analysis is still true. The only thing absolutely true is what appears as a datum, something given to my consciousness. Maybe things are not as they appear, but the appearance is always well known for me. Maybe the lake I am perceiving is a hallucination, but the appearance of the lake is always true for me. The phenomenological method is just to describe how things appear to us, the rest is mere speculation.

Positivism is usually characterized as a radicalization of human knowledge, by which only sense experience is accepted as valid. But Husserl claims that phenomenology is a more radical positivism than the classical one. Phenomenology only accepts as true what is positively given regardless of the origin. What is positively given is the phenomenon, the datum for consciousness, the appearance. This idea leads Husserl to claim that he is the most radical positivist.

2. Eidetic Reduction

2.1. Two Kinds of Intuitions

As we saw before, freedom of presupposition implies the suspension of our knowledge on authority, tradition, and positive science. This means that phenomenology must be reduced to a nucleus in which authority, tradition and positive science are placed into brackets. The real freedom of presuppositions is a way of liberation of prejudices to remain in the area of pure data of consciousness. *A phenomenologist only accepts what is given immediately to his consciousness*, which is the sphere of evidence. How things themselves are given is the same as how things themselves are data for my consciousness.[2] Now, is not what is given immediately to the consciousness just what is given to empirical experience? This is only partly true, because that this is the only mode of giveness to consciousness is something that has to be investigated. Empiricism and positivism holds that the only thing immediately given to consciousness is sense experience. Husserl contends this claim.

The only valid beginning, free of presuppositions, is to start from the pure datum given to consciousness, and it is a fact perceived in internal experience that the only experience of what is immediately given is not only empirical experience but also intellectual experience (see categorial intuition in Chapter 2, Section 5.4). Experience is the source of everything contingent, subject to change in time, but it is evident to us that we know things that are not subject to contingency, they are necessary. For example, the scientific fact that "green plants perform photosynthesis" is subject to contingency; it depends on the constitution of our world, and it is subject to refutation by an experience that contradicts it. On the contrary, the Pythagorean theorem "$a^2+b^2=c^2$" is true necessarily, regardless of the constitution of the existing world, and there is nothing in the real world that could possibly refute it. This shows that we have two kinds of knowledge. The first is the empirical experience; the second an intellectual experience. To these two kinds of knowledge correspond two kinds of evidence, empirical and intellectual.

An important step is that the intellectual knowledge accompanies all our empirical knowledge, in other words, the contingency and individuality of what is given in empirical experience is ruled by what is given in intellectual experience: "it belongs to the sense of anything contingent to having an essence and therefore an Eidos which can be apprehended purely."[3] The essence or *eidos* of any empirical datum has the character of necessity over against the contingency of the pure empirical datum. For example, this individual tree that I am perceiving at this moment is contingent. It could not be, or it could change if it is not changing. But the essence of tree, its *eidos*, is always the same. The essence of tree has always and necessarily the same properties even if there are no trees anymore, whether I am dreaming, or whether I am having some hallucination. Essences or eidos are like numbers and mathematical equations, they have necessary and absolute validity.

What Husserl calls "the eidetic reduction" is precisely the reduction of any empirical datum to its eidos, to its essence, to its necessary ideal conditions. The eidetic reduction is the intuition or insight of the eidos of everything with evidence.

When we perceive an object we are having simultaneously two intuitions, an empirical one by which an individual is given originally, and an eidetic one by which an eidos or essence (a universal object according to the terminology of *Logical Investigation*) is given

44

originally as well.[4] Therefore, there are two well-differentiated modes of being given: intuition of individuals and intuition of essences (ideation). In reality, one implies the other and vice versa: "Certainly, in consequence of that, no intuition of essence is possible without the free possibility of turning one's regard to a 'corresponding' individual and forming a consciousness of an example — just as, conversely, no intuition of something individual is possible without the free possibility of bringing about an ideation and, in it, directing one's regard to the corresponding essence exemplified in what is individually sighted."[5] We have here, then, that "the essence (eidos) is a new sort of object. Just as the datum of a sense intuition is an individual object, so the datum of an eidetic intuition is a pure essence."[6] Both objects are given originally, in person, to the respective experiences. Individual facts are the road to their eidos, but eidos, essences or universal objects do not include any affirmation about existence, individual facts, etc.[7] The eidos or essence of tree, for example, contains no affirmation about the existence of trees, as it was said, it could be that there are no trees any more, but the essence tree will be still true. There are essences that do not have any actual individual, but all eidos or essence has at least the possibility of being instantiated in the imagination.

The distinction between empirical intuition and eidetic intuition is the origin of two classes of sciences. The empirical intuition is the base for the so-called empirical sciences, and the eidetic intuition is the base for the eidetic sciences.[8]

2.2. The Method of Eidetic Reduction

When we perceive an individual object, we simultaneously have an intuition of its essence; we know that such an object belongs to a kind, an eidos. For example, in the perception of this individual horse the concept horse, its natural kind, is apprehended or intuited as well. If we do not know that what we are perceiving belongs to the universal kind horse, we would not know that what we perceive is a horse. Now, in all these cases, the eidos is given along with the individual. How do we separate the eidos from the individual fact? Eidetic Reduction is precisely the method to isolate the Eidos from the individual fact. *Eidetic Reduction consists of producing variations in the individual object until we see what is invariable in it.* What is invariable is its essence or eidos. The obvious way to produce these variations is by perceiving the individual object from different sides, manipulating the object, using past experiences of the individual object, and if it is possible, building a model to try new modifications until we have invariable properties of that object, properties that are equally valid for all the individuals of a certain kind.

Nevertheless, this procedure is in some way impractical. Husserl —following the same idea from Brentano in his *Descriptive Psychology*— suggests using our imagination and fantasy as a substitution for the real object. With our fantasy we can vary at will all the elements of the individual object, eliminating what is purely individual of the object, and retaining what is invariable, essential to the object. In this method, "free fantasy acquires a position of primacy over perceptions."[9] Fantasy is not restricted to a model as is the case in external perception; in fantasy we have incomparably more freedom reshaping at will the figures feigned or fantasized, and in running through continuously modified possible shapes and forms. Fantasy is so important for the eidetic reduction that Husserl goes as far as to say that "feigning makes up the vital element of phenomenology."[10] It is obvious that Husserl (and before him, his master Brentano) was inspired by the procedure of geometry, which arrives to the eidos of geometrical formation by the play of fantasy.

Once we have the clear evidence of the eidos of an object, the intellectual intuition of the eidos, the next step is the formulation of the a priori laws that are based on this eidos. Let us see this aspect of the eidetic reduction.

When we grasp an essence after the eidetic reduction, we also grasp the necessary essential laws grounded in it. Once we grasped the eidos or essence, the necessary essential laws are not dependent on the actual existence of the observed or imagined instances in which they intuit an essence or eidos. In this sense, Husserl thinks that we have an *a priori* knowledge of necessary essences. In other words, once we know the eidos of an instance, this essence will be valid both for all my future or possible experiences of such objects, whether they exist in the real world, or were to exist in any possible world.

For example, when I grasp the essence or eidos of a tree, I know that the essential moments (parts) of the eidos tree (kind of reproduction, metabolism, growth, composition, etc.) apply not only to the actual world, but to any real and possible world, and to any real and possible instance of tree. I know that the irreducible datum which we call "tree" cannot and could not exist, anywhere or at any time, without implying that kind of reproduction, metabolism, growth, composition, etc., which are the moments of the essence of tree.

Let us see a counterexample to see what Husserl has in mind. Assume that we found an object, similar to what we call "tree," but instead of being made of carbon is made of another element called "Germanium." The eidetic reduction of this instance would yield an essence or eidos that is different from the other made of carbon, which was a moment of the eidos of tree. So, the object made of Germanion is not a case under the eidos tree. Notice that it is very important which essential moments we grasp from an instance in an eidetic intuition. Sometimes, we grasp a few essential moments of an instance that are not enough to differentiate from another instance. The problem should be resolved by describing better the instances, using the imaginative manipulation in order to exhaust all possibilities. But the eidos grasped in either case will have essential laws that are not-dependent on facts.

A caveat: One of the most extended criticisms against phenomenology is precisely about the eidetic intuition. It is said that we cannot know the real essence of a thing just by analyzing our consciousness (our consciousness of an object). How is it possible, for example, to know the essence of water (H_2O) simply by analyzing the appearance of water to my consciousness? The answer is clear. No, we cannot know the essence of a thing just by analyzing our consciousness of that thing. *The eidetic intuition is not about real essences but ideal essences.* Phenomenology does not attempt to substitute any of the actual sciences at all. By using the eidetic reduction, phenomenology wants to indicate the necessary conditions for certain objects, but this is very different from knowing the real essences of extramental things.

3. Phenomenological Reduction

3.1. The Method of Phenomenological Reduction

In order to arrive to the authentic freedom of presuppositions, the phenomenologist has to perform a more radical reduction, what Husserl called with various expressions, namely, *epoché*, phenomenological reduction, or transcendental reduction. The term "*epoché*" is a Greek word that means the suspension of judgement, abstention. For the Greek sceptic, the *epoché* was the philosophical result of doubting and a way of philosophical life. Descartes used the same idea, but not as a way of philosophical life but as a method to start philosophizing; that is to say, Descartes used methodical doubt only in the beginning of his philosophizing. Husserl agrees only partially with the Greek sceptics and Descartes about the use of the *epoché*. (i) Husserl uses *epoché* in the original sense of the Greek sceptics, but for Husserl, *epoché* is a method and not a conclusion. (ii) Husserl's *epoché* is not the Cartesian doubt nor an attempt to doubt.[11] The phenomenological *epoché* is a method to be used all the time, and not only at the beginning. It does not put in question what is in suspension (as Descartes does), but what is suspended is only separated without rejecting it in order to have immediate and evident access to the data of consciousness.

The phenomenological *epoché* is just a bracketing or a disconnection, the abstention of judging of the existence. This does not mean that a phenomenologist doubts the existence of facts, but purely and simply that factual existence is put out of action as a method to achieve a presuppositionless philosophy. The phenomenological *epoché* place into brackets the existential facts and leaves only the *phenomenon*, what is given for consciousness. The phenomenological reduction is just the reduction of every thing to its phenomenon, which is the appearance, and all appearance is something that is for consciousness. For example, the tree that I am perceiving now is reduced to a mere phenomenon for my consciousness, and to achieve this, I parenthesize the existence of this tree. What will remain is only the appearance to me, an appearance that is not only a sense appearance but intellectual one as well. This reduction to what appears to me is called phenomenon.

Husserl claims that with the phenomenological reduction one does not lose any of the properties of the nature of the object. The existential tree has the same properties (green, tall, vegetative life, and so on) as the tree after the phenomenological reduction. (100 actual dollars have the same number as 100 fictitious dollars). But there is an important difference: what I see, perceive, and understand as phenomenon is absolutely evident for me regardless of whether the object exists or not. Nobody can question seriously what I am seeing or understanding as an immediate datum for my consciousness.

3.2. Natural and Phenomenological Attitude

Husserl calls "natural attitude" the spontaneous attitude of human consciousness, which is oriented to the world and affirms its existence. The effect of the *epoché* is to put this natural attitude out of action, to exclude this natural attitude from consciousness, to put into brackets the existential thesis of the natural attitude. After the phenomenological *epoché*, the natural world of the natural attitude becomes a pure datum for consciousness, a phenomenon.

Husserl calls "phenomenological attitude" (or transcendental attitude) the reflective attitude, which has as its object the conscious life, the ways in which things are given to consciousness. The phenomenological attitude is the result of the *epoché*. As it was established before, the phenomenological method is a reflection on the structure *ego cogito cogitatum*. The *epoché* exercises this reflection in which all existing things of the world become purely *cogitata*, something merely thought by our consciousness.

In natural attitude I do not make the subject of interest that *I am*

48

knowing an object. In natural attitude I am simply living in the certainty of the existence of the object (this is the thesis of the natural attitude). In phenomenological attitude I direct my interest to the fact that *I am thinking an object*. The object is contemplated *only* in relation to my act of thinking and my ego. The object is not seen as an independent being in the world, but as something dependent on my mental act of thinking. The object that depends on my act of thinking is called "phenomenon," or in the terminology of *Logical Investigations*, "intentional object." In summary, the *epoché* directs my attention (exercises the reflection) to the structure *ego—cogito—cogitatum*.

Let us see an example to illustrate this point. In natural attitude I perceive this tree as an existing thing in front of me, with a certain color, shape, and other properties. The *epoché* excludes this natural world by parenthesizing the worldly existence in space and time. In reality, what the *epoché* is doing is reflecting on my experience of perceiving the tree, and in doing this, I do not take the tree as an existing thing but as the counter-pole of my experience, as the terminus of my intentional act, that is to say, as a mere phenomenon for my consciousness. So, the phenomenological attitude is a reflection on "I-perceive-the-perceived-tree" (a particular case of *ego cogito cogitatum*). Take into consideration that here one is not reflecting on the existing tree but on one's experience of perceiving the tree. And because the act of perceiving has the essential property of intentionality, when I experience my own experience of perception, I am automatically transported to its intentional object tree. This is the same thing as to say that the tree was reduced into a pure phenomenon for my consciousness. The tree loses its space-temporal existence to become a purely mental datum.

From the perspective of the phenomenological attitude, it is easy to understand why Husserl calls the natural attitude a "dogmatic attitude". While one remains in the natural attitude, one is unable to effect criticism on oneself; one is just accepting what is given in natural attitude regardless of evidence. It is just accepted by natural inclination.

Husserl believes that the thinker who remains in natural attitude presupposes important ontological commitments, which are ultimately responsible for its philosophical naivety. These commitments are the existence of physical objects, the existence of their properties, causal relations, etc. It seems obvious that if these ontological commitments are the cause of the uncritical dogmatism and naivety, then a method to remove these commitments seems to be necessary. The *epoché* becomes the procedure to eliminate these commitments presupposed in natural attitude. Thus, instead of remaining in this attitude, Husserl proposes to alter it radically, to neutralize the natural thesis, the ontological commitment of the natural attitude, and this neutralization gives rise to the phenomenological attitude, the sphere of absolute evidence.

There are strong similarities between these ideas and Meinong's notion of the prejudice toward reality. As is well known, Husserl and Meinong had difficult professional relationships, although both were students of Brentano at the same time. Meinong introduced the "prejudice toward the real" (the natural bias for the real world in detriment of irreality) to develop his theory of objects, in which the notion of object implies what is real and unreal, present, past and future, what is existing and nonexisting, possible and impossible. So, the notion of object is infinitely wider than reality. What Husserl calls "natural attitude" or "dogmatic attitude" is what Meinong calls "prejudice toward the real." Nevertheless, Husserl did not mention these similarities.

3.3. Phenomenological Reductions

The phenomenological attitude implies several phenomenological reductions.

(1) The exclusion of nature is the methodical means that makes the turning of regard to transcendentally pure consciousness possible. The exclusion of the natural world implies "the physical and psychophysical world, all individual objectivities which become constituted by axiological and practical functioning of consciousness, ... all the sorts of cultural formations, all works of the technical and fine arts, ... aesthetic and practical values of every form. ... Consequently, all natural sciences and cultural sciences."[12]

(2) Human beings as natural beings are excluded as well. This implies that the natural ego, the psychological ego, the existential ego is also excluded. What remains is the *pure ego*, or transcendental ego. Now, Husserl goes further; what about the pure Ego? Did this ego or phenomenological ego become a transcendental nothing because of the phenomenological reduction or *epoché*? Let us see what Husserl himself says about this: "After carrying out this reduction we shall not encounter the pure Ego anywhere in the flux of manifold mental processes which remain as a transcendental residuum —neither as one mental process among others, nor strictly a part of a mental process, arising and then disappearing with the mental process of which it is a part. The Ego seems to be there continually, indeed, necessarily, and this continuity is obviously not that of a stupidly persistent mental process, a 'fixed idea.' Instead, *the Ego belongs to each coming and*

50

going mental process; its 'regard' is directed 'through' each actional cogito to the objective something. This ray of each new cogito from one cogito to the next, shooting forth anew with each new cogito and vanishing with it. The Ego, however, is something identical. At least, considered eidetically, any cogito can change, come and go, even though one may doubt that every cogito is necessarily something transitory and not simply, as we find it, something in fact transitory. In contradistinction, the pure Ego would, however, seem to be something essentially necessary and, as something absolutely identical throughout every actual or possible change in the mental process, *it cannot in any sense be a really inherent part or moment of the mental process itself.*"[13]

Keeping in mind the essential structure of phenomenology (*ego cogito cogitatum*), we can say that every mental act (every cogito, as Husserl says) belongs to the ego, and the ego belongs to every mental act. All mental processes, the stream of mental acts, belong to the one stream of mental processes, which is mine. The pure ego is just a residuum after performing the phenomenological reduction of both the natural world and the empirical subjectivity included in the natural world.

The pure Ego is at the same time immanent to the stream of mental processes and transcendent to it. As Husserl puts it, "a transcendence within immanence." The pure ego is *immanent* or it belongs to the stream of consciousness, but at the same time is transcendent because it is a residuum which is not subject to be reduced to the mere stream of consciousness nor become a mere phenomenon. The pure ego escapes the standard reduction and remains a residuum. We will talk more about this in the next chapter.

(3) The transcendence pertaining to God falls under the phenomenological reduction as well. "The existence of an extra-worldly 'divine' being is that this being would obviously transcend not merely the world but 'absolute' consciousness. ... We extend the phenomenological reduction to include this ... being. It shall remain excluded from the new field of research ... of pure consciousness."[14] Again, this does not mean that the phenomenologist rejects, doubts or affirms the existence of God, but that the transcendence of God is methodologically excluded.

(4) The phenomenological reduction excludes all transcendencies. Now, eidetic objects, universal objects, essences, etc, are also transcendent to pure consciousness in some sense. Universal objects are not part of the natural world as real parts because they are ideal in character. But universal objects are transcendent to consciousness in some sense because they are not real parts of the stream of

51

consciousness either. Nevertheless, the phenomenologist cannot go on excluding transcendencies without limit. The transcendental purification of the *epoché* does not mean an exclusion of all transcendencies because a science of pure consciousness would not be possible. If we exclude all eidetic objects, universals, meanings, etc., we will exclude all eidetic sciences as well, among them phenomenology. Let us see this with some detail.

Husserl distinguishes between material ontologies and formal ontologies. The phenomenological reduction is performed over the material ontologies but not over the formal ontologies. Material ontologies are the ontologies of things. An ontology of nature belongs to physical nature; an ontology of psychophysical being belongs to the psychophysical, and in general, metaphysics is considered a material ontology. All these disciplines are subject under the *epoché*. Formal ontologies are the formal and logical conditions for the material ontologies. For example, the notion of object in general is part of a formal ontology, but a material thing, or a psychological process, is part of a material ontology. Objects, in the sense of intentional objects or objects for a consciousness, are always present regardless of the existence of material things. This table is an object for my consciousness (an intentional object) regardless of whether I am perceiving this table, I am dreaming of this table, or I am having a hallucination. In all these cases, the object is the formal condition and part of the formal ontology. Concepts, propositions, universals, formal logic, and in general the eidetic world, are part of the formal ontology. Husserl notices that even the mental processes are also subsumed under the logically broadest sense of the term "object." Therefore, we are unable to exclude formal logic and formal ontology.

Nevertheless, Husserl recognizes that in some sense it is possible to exclude formal ontology and formal logic from the phenomenological attitude. What remains will be the descriptive analysis of data given in pure and immediate intuition. In this sense, neither logic, nor mathematical disciplines will be of use to phenomenology. The only thing that remains is pure intuition and the description of what is given to pure intuition, in other words, to accept nothing but what we can see as essentially evident by observing consciousness itself. So, here we have a more purified definition of phenomenology:

> Phenomenology D*f*.= A purely eidetic-descriptive discipline that explores the field of transcendentally pure consciousness by pure intuition.

Now, can a phenomenologist exclude absolutely all logic? Not at all. The only propositions of logic to which phenomenology can count on are logical axioms such as the law of contradiction and its derivations.[15]

In summary, what is the effect of the *epoché*? The sphere of what is transcendental. What is the scope of the transcendental field? Pure experiences, that is to say, pure consciousness with its pure correlates: the *cogitata* and the *cogito*, and with this, the *ego*. What remains is the structure *Ego Cogito Cogitatum*.

3.4. The Principle of All Principles

Empiricism and positivism take as their basic principle the adherence to what is given, the return to things in themselves. As we saw, Husserl accepts this principle but not without important modifications about both what is given and what is the meaning of a return to things in themselves.

Husserl does not accept empiricism but accepts the principle of the given. This principle is not only the origin of any science or theory, but no conceivable theory can make us err with respect of this principle. Husserl formulates the principle of all principles in the following way: "every originary intuitive presentation is a legitimizing source of knowledge," and more explicitly, "everything originally (so to speak, in its personal actuality) offered to us in intuition is to be accepted simply as what is presented as being, but also only within the limits in which it is presented here."[16]

The principle of all principles is the absolute evidence of what is given in intuition. Intuition is not only empirical intuition (empiricism and positivism) but also intellectual intuition of essences. Intuition is like seeing the object in person. There is a seeing of empirical objects in person, and there is also a seeing of eidetic structures, essences of things in person, as we saw before. "Seeing essences is an originary presenting act and, as a presenting act, is the analogue of sense perceiving and not of imagining."[17]

The problem here comes, as Husserl points out, when we judge these claims from the point of view of empiricism. An empiricist accepts the principle of intuition, but intuition restricted to empirical experience, for the empiricist considers dogmatically that essences are pure fictions. But this is not what appears in the description of what is given to me in intuition. It is evident that there are objects given in person by means of sense experience —regardless of whether these objects exist or not. We have here the phenomenon of something given directly or in person. Now, it is evident, too, that there are objects given in person, directly, by means of intellectual experience — the essences of things. I do not have experience that these essences are

53

produced by me, or are a result of fiction activity. What I experience is that they are given to me directly, in person. I do not know what is the origin of these essences; the only thing I know for sure, in complete evidence, is that they are present to me in person. On the contrary, when I feign or create an image, I experience that I am producing that image; I am conscious of its constructive origin, something that does not appear in intuition when I have the experience of an essence. So, the empiricist is just theorizing and speculating about the fictional character of essences, without giving any justification for it.

The empiricist misses the important distinction between *experiences that are spontaneous* such as intuitions and *experiences that are arbitrary* such as imagination. In the description of what is given, some objects are experienced spontaneously (sensuous objects and essences), while others are experienced as arbitrarily produced (fictions).

We have here two kinds of very different experiences or presentations:

(1) *Originary presentation.* This is the intuition, in which an object is presented originally, directly, in person. The subjective characteristic of this experience is its *spontaneity.* There are two sorts of intuitions:

(a) *Sense intuition,* by which a sensuous object is given in person.

(b) *Intellectual intuition* or ideation, by which the essence or eidetic structure of an object is given originally or in person. The intuition of essences is a spontaneous experience, not a creative experience as the empiricist believes dogmatically.

(2) *Arbitrary presentations.* The object is not given in person or directly but by means of an arbitrary activity. We notice that they were created by our own mental activity. We are conscious of its production; we experience that they are constructs, something that we cannot say of the intuition of essences.

It is important to remember what was mentioned several times, all these analyses are not concerned with the reality of the object. A phenomenologist is only concerned with phenomena, what is immediately given. To intuit an object does not mean, then, that this object exists, but only that it is present to my consciousness in a certain way. Husserl is only analyzing the most originary and primary source of our knowledge before the arrival of any theory. Any human knowledge, the most sophisticated theory, must be founded, in the end, on intuitions, otherwise that knowledge and that sophisticated theory would be purely and simply dogmatism. Husserl's phenomenology is only concerned with these origins in order to prepare a solid foundation for any science. In other words, all human knowledge can be traced back to its origins, and here we have only the evidence of seeing, otherwise, all knowledge is constructed on nothing. To go to the origins of our knowledge, Husserl suggested a method of reduction that leads us to our primitive and originary data of consciousness, where we can justify a statement by replying "I see that it is so," that is to say, I see intuitively that something is directly given to me.

In Husserl's words: "If we see an object with full clarity, if we have carried out processes of discrimination and conceptual comprehension purely on the basis of the seeing and within the limits of what is actually seized upon in seeing, if we then see ... how the object is, the faithful expressive statement has, as a consequence, its legitimacy. Not to assign any value to "I see it" as an answer to the question, "Why?" would be a countersense."[18]

The reduction, like Descartes's methodical doubt, has the task of eliminating what is not directly evident in our knowledge and arriving to what is necessary or apodictic. The most radical reduction is the *epoché*, by which all our knowledge is reduced to a phenomenon for our consciousness. Here, no theory can make us err because we are only dealing with what is directly appearing to our consciousness. For example, the object "red spot" in natural attitude implies being committed to the existence of this color, something that may be problematic, but reduced to a mere phenomenon for my consciousness, reduced to pure datum to my consciousness, the red spot is something that truly appears to me regardless of the failure of my senses, the scientific explanation, and the problematicity of its existence. No one can contest that what I am seeing is a red spot, even if the red spot does not exist, because I am not talking about the existence of the red spot but the appearance to me, the phenomenon. In this sense, what is given in intuition is the principle of all principles.

3.5. Evidence and Intuition

As it is easy to conclude from our aforementioned analyses, there is a close connection between the character of given, intuition and evidence. As we saw in the preceding section, there are two modes of the given: (i) originary giveness or intuition, and (ii) non-originary giveness such as the arbitrariness of feigning. The term "originary" means that there is no further origin of something. For example, the perception of a landscape is a case of intuition or originary giveness because the phenomenon of landscape does not have another origin than its very presence to me. On the contrary, the recollection of a landscape is a case of non-originary giveness because the phenomenon of landscape has another origin, another further source in a past perception. Both modes of the given are modes of consciousness; we are conscious of this; that is to say, this is not a theory, an speculation, but an immediate experience.

The two modes of the given are sources of epistemological justification that are closely related to the evidence and its modes.

Husserl distinguishes two kinds of evidence: (i) Originary assertoric evidence which occurs in external perception, and (ii) originary apodictic evidence which occurs in our immanent conscious experience. These two kinds of evidence have important consequences for phenomenology.

The originary assertoric evidence, which is found in external perception, implies the following characteristics: (i) it is evidence of what is contingent in character, and (ii) it is inadequate evidence because the object is given in successive appearances to infinity. The perception of this tree is given to my consciousness in successive sides, first in front, then back, up, etc. There are infinite sides, and none of them exhausts the object. Husserl calls "transcendent given" this mode of the given because it refers to an X, something outside of consciousness. But because this evidence is not adequate, the perception of something transcendent is doubtful.

The originary apodictic evidence implies: (i) evidence of what is absolute and necessary, and (ii) an adequate evidence because the object is given without sides. The originary apodictic evidence occurs inside the life of consciousness, where our experiences are given to us with all their moments and intentional elements. Husserl calls "immanent given" this mode of the given because the datum for consciousness is a unity with the giving act. In other words, following Brentano's view on inner perception, Husserl accepts that *every experience, every act is in principle perceptible in reflection*. Because this evidence is adequate, the perception of something immanent is indubitable, *incorrigibile*. The stream of mental processes which is mine, no matter to what extent it is not grasped, as soon as I look at the flowing life in its actual present, I apprehend myself as the pure subject of this life. "I say unqualifiedly and necessarily, that I am, this life is, I am living: *cogito*."[19]

I apprehend my own self in originary evidence: "Over against the positing of the world, which is a contingent positing, there stands then the positing of my pure Ego and Ego-life which is a necessary, absolutely indubitable positing. Anything physical which is given in person can be non-existing, no mental process which is given in person can be non-existing."[20]   But evidence is of diverse clarity, there are modes of clarity of evidence.

There is a direct relationship between modes of being given, intuition and degrees of clarity of evidence. As one has noticed in this analysis, "being given" is tantamount to saying "being apprehended." So, modes of clarity of evidence will be the result of modes of being apprehended (apprehended in fantasy, in perception, eidetic intuition, etc.) There are degrees of clarity and a process of clarification from what is obscure to what is clear. Now, if we are conscious of this process of clarification, it means that obscurity is already a certain mode of being given, a mode of being apprehended. How is this possible? It is phenomenologically evident that all our experiences are given with other experiences. There are no independent experiences; [21] every experience that falls under the scope of our *cogito* is given with the backdrop of other experiences that are its horizon until reaching the originary horizon of the pure Ego. Obscurity and clarity are given in adequate evidence, so we are dealing with necessary evidence. On the contrary, external perception is inadequate evidence, so we have only assertoric evidence.

The last analysis is very important, because phenomenology can exclude no datum however obscurely it is given. "Immediate 'seeing,' not merely sensuous, experiential seeing, but seeing in the universal sense as an originally presenting consciousness of any kind whatsoever, is *the ultimate legitimizing source of all rational assertions*."[22] Here Husserl means that the most characteristic seeing of phenomenology is the universal seeing, eidetic intuition after having performed the *epoché*, by which any object is given in some eidos, in some universal or kind. There is eidetic intuition of our natural world, any external object can be seen in an eidos. Thus, the natural world given in external perception is just a case of the possible natural worlds that can exemplify that eidos. There can be many possible variations that are cases of the same eidos. But, the eidos, the essence of the object, is given with adequate evidence (is given *immediately* and without sides), that is to say, we have necessary evidence of the essence of the object. The same can be said of our conscious life. Phenomenology is interested in the eidos of our mental life. Because of this relationship between eidos and its cases, Husserl claims that there is an *a priori* knowledge of the possible empirical knowledge, and this gives rise to what Husserl calls "regional ontologies," which are the *a priori* regions under which the empirical world is subsumed, the *a priori* conditions, the eidetic conditions for the constitution (the given or being apprehended) of the world.[23]

ENDNOTES

[1] Edmund Husserl, *Ideas Pertaining to a Pure Phenomenology and to a Phenomenological Philosoiphy*, First Book [quoted as *Ideas I*], translated by F. Kersten, Dordrecht, Kluwer Academic Publishers, 1982, § 63.

[2] Husserl, *Ideas I*, § 19.

[3] Husserl, *Ideas I*, § 2.

[4] Cf. Husserl, *Ideas I*, § 3.

[5] Husserl, *Ideas I*, § 3.

[6] Husserl, *Ideas I*, § 3.

[7] Cf. Husserl, *Ideas I*, § 5.

[8] Cf. Husserl, *Ideas I*, § 7.

[9] Husserl, *Ideas I*, § 70.

[10] Husserl, *Ideas I*, § 70.

[11] Cf. Husserl, *Ideas I*, § 31.

[12] Husserl, *Ideas I*, § 56.

[13] Husserl, *Ideas I*, § 57.

[14] Husserl, *Ideas I*, § 58.

[15] Cf. Husserl, *Ideas I*, § 59.

[16] Husserl, *Ideas I*, § 24.

[17] Husserl, *Ideas I*, § 23.

[18] Husserl, *Ideas I*, § 19.

[19] Husserl, *Ideas I*, § 46.

[20] Husserl, *Ideas I*, § 46.

[21] Cf. Husserl, *Ideas I*, § 83.

[22] Husserl, *Ideas* § 19.

[23] Cf. Husserl, *Ideas I*, § 149.

4

Transcendental Phenomenology

1. Transcendental Reduction

The term "phenomenology" is very closely related to phenomenological reduction. There are different sorts of phenomenological reduction and, as a consequence, different sorts of phenomenology. Let us see these two kinds of reductions, in which we are now interested:

(1) Phenomenological reduction as *epoché* on "positing-the-being." This *epoché* concerns things and the natural world. Here the phenomenologist puts out of action the general thesis of the natural attitude, he places between brackets everything this thesis embraces (the existence of the entire natural world). This phenomenological reduction is what was developed in Husserl's *Ideas I*. This sort of reduction, called in general "*epoché*" is Cartesian in character (putting out of action all the transcendent positings).

(2) Phenomenological reduction as *epoché* on the self, that is to say, a transcendental reduction (or transcendental *epoché*), which gives rise to transcendental phenomenology. The transcendental reduction neutralizes the "ontic residue" of a consciousness conceived psychologically, namely, with a real stream of consciousness. "*Epoché* allows me a universal reflection on my self-being ... The transcendental *epoché* is therefore such an 'overturning' of the self steadily living through its life-acts which in his straightforward attitude to the world he intuits as his ever new will to live."[1] This *epoché* concerns the self and its being as the will to live.

Both phenomenological reductions are clearly connected, but separated in tasks. "A universal inhibition from all 'taking-up-positions' such that we may call it 'phenomenological *epoché*' at once becomes the methodical means by which I catch myself as a pure 'I' Every mundane being and every thing in space and time is for me insofar as I experience or perceive it."[2] *The phenomenological*

*reduction not only embraces the reduction of the natural world but
also the psychological ego as something real.* We can formulate the
general idea of phenomenological reduction which embraces the two
aforementioned tasks in the following formula:

> Phenomenological Reduction =Df. Bracketing existence and
> that of keeping in suspense any transcendent validity of our
> knowledge-claims, which include both the transcendency of
> the world and our ego.

Although there is a unity between both phenomenological
reductions, transcendental reduction introduces an important attitude.
From a phenomenological point of view, the *epoché* on the natural
world maintains all the essential elements of the world, that is to say,
by bracketing the existence nothing new is produced in the world. The
methodological elimination of existence from the world keeps the same
properties. Between this existing tree and the tree reduced to a
phenomenon for my consciousness there is no difference in properties;
any property we describe in the phenomenon can be found in the real
tree. On the contrary, the transcendental reduction of the self yields a
new attitude, which manifests the maximal intensity of
phenomenological attitude because the phenomenologist inhibits his
general interest in mundane things. The reflection is not interested in
intentional objects but in the life of the ego.

The result of this phenomenological attitude is a reflection on the
experience (*cogito*) in which the phenomenologist distinguishes the
intentional object (*cogitatum*) and the ego, and thus we have again the
main axle of phenomenology and object of the phenomenological
reflection: *ego cogito cogitatum.* In other words, the experience
(*cogito*) manifests itself as having a two-direction polarity: the
cogitatum of the *cogito* (what is thought as thought, the intentional
object) and the ego of the *cogito.* This unity of the structure *ego
cogito cogitatum* implies that there is no intentional object (*cogitatum*)
without experience (*cogito*), and there is no ego without experience
(*cogito*).[3] With transcendental reduction, the phenomenologist is
oriented toward the ego.

2. The Essential Components of Mental Processes: Noesis and Noema

Phenomenology studies a mental process or experience as such,
that is to say, eidetically, in its essence, which is the result of the
eidetic reduction. The components of a mental process eidetically

considered is a unity of meaning (we already knew that the eidetic unity was a unity of meaning as was explained in *Logical Investigations*). In this unity of meaning Husserl distinguishes three components: (i) the meaning, (ii) what is endowed with meaning, and (iii) the operation that endows the meaning (the meaning-conferring act). What is endowed with meaning is sensuous material data, which Husserl calls "*hyle*" (a Greek term meaning "matter"). The operation that endows the meaning Husserl now calls "noesis," which confers the meaning to the *hyle*, and the meaning is called "noema," which leads us to what is transcendent to consciousness. Only the noema and the noesis are essential components.

Let us see an example offered by Husserl.[4] Suppose that we regard with pleasure a blossoming apple tree. We have two situations. (i) In the natural attitude, the apple tree is something existing, a transcendent thing, and the psychological state of pleasure is also something actual belonging to real people. In this attitude we find real relations among the objects of the world, and other relations between the perceiver and the perceived objects of the world. If we are undergoing a hallucination, then the apple tree does not exist. The relations between objects and persons do not exist either; only the person who perceives and undergoes the hallucination exists. (ii) In the phenomenological attitude the whole transcendent world is placed into brackets; we exercise the *epoché* in relation to the actual being of the world. The existing relations between objects and perceiver is bracketed as well. The only thing that is left over is the experience (*cogito*), which has an intention to the corresponding intentional object (the *cogitatum*) and the ego. (Remember that all intentional experience implies the intentional object). The intentional object of apple tree maintains all the characteristics that the actual apple tree has. The intentional object of the essence of the apple tree (not the actual apple tree) is the noema. The noema is given by the conscious act, experience or noesis of the apple tree. The noesis reduces the sense data to the unity of meaning. The sense datum is called by Husserl "*hyle*," which is the color of the apple tree, tactile sensations of the apple tree, shape, etc. The noesis gives the meaning (noema) to the *hyle*; it reduces the plurality of sense material (*hyle*) to the unity of the noema.

In this example, the elements noesis and *hyle* are *immanent* ingredients of the experience. However, the noema is not an immanent ingredient of the experience but the intentional correlate. In this sense, the noema is transcendent to the experience, but it is not transcendent as the natural world is transcendent. The noema —we can say— is immanent in relation to the (unreduced) natural world, but it is transcendent to the experience because the idea of apple tree (in Husserl's example) is not an integral part of the experience.

This implies three areas of phenomenological research: (i) phenomenology of *hyle* (phenomenology of sense content), (ii) phenomenology of the noesis (the experience or act of consciousness), and (iii) phenomenology of the noema (the eidetic content of the intentional object). According to Husserl, the most important part of phenomenology is the analysis of noesis.[5] The reason for this is that Husserl is more concerned with (a) how the noesis constitutes the noema, how conscious acts constitute the objectivities, and (b) carrying out an eidetic analysis of the noesis, and to describe the essential laws that appear between these eidetic contents of noesis. Notice (something that is already obvious) that Husserl constantly views the noesis as acts that have the characteristic of intentionality, they always refer to the corresponding noema. Although the noesis is the most important analysis of phenomenology, the noema is always present, and the ego accompanies the performance of the cogito; so, the description of the cogito implies the description of the cogitatum and the ego. Nevertheless, in this stage of the phenomenological analysis, the correlation noesis and noema is the most important in the phenomenological analysis.[6]

Husserl analyzes the noema and found at least three divisions within it that mirror the activitis of the noesis. This paralellism between noema and noesis is because there is an correlation between noema and noesis, which Husserl calls "principle of *a priori* correlation," by which differences in the noema have an *a priori* interconnection or link in the noesis, and vice versa. "A parallelism between noesis and noema is indeed thecase, but it is such that one must describe the formation on both sides and in their essentially mutual correspondence."[7]

(This principle is another way of expression that mental acts are specified by their objects and the objects are intended by their mental acts, a principle that Brentano used in the classification of mental phenomena, and he took from medieval philosophy).

There are three moments or parts within the noema:

(1) *A pure substrate of predicates*, that is, the pure X in abstraction from which it is said all predicates. "Theidentical intentional object becomes [...] distinguished from the changing and

alterable predicates. It becomes separated as central noematic moment: the object [...], the identical, the determinable subject of its predicates—a pure X in abstraction from all predicates—and it becomes separated from these predicates or, more precisely, from the predicate-noemas."[8]

(2) *The noematic sense*, (*Sinn*), that is, the sheer objective meaning, or central nucleous of characteristics, which is the X filled out by the corresponding predicates. It is the definite system of predicates that determine the content of the core of the noema.

(3) *The quality*, which is the mode of presentation of the object: the object as seen, perceived, desired, recalled, hallucinated, etc.

Although Husserl divides the noema into three moments, these together constitute the complete noema. The noema is not only the sense (*Sinn*) but the X of reference of the predicates and the quality. This description of what is noema makes impossible to equate Husserl's noema with Frege's sense. The latter is just a moment of the former. But there are more important differences.

Certainly, Husserl's sense (*Sinn*) and Frege's sense have interesting similarities: for both philosophers, sense is a way of being directed to an object. Husserl explicitly writes: "Each noema has a content, that is to say, its sense, and is related through it to its object,"[9] a statement that Frege could agree. Now, it is unfear to compare Husserl's notion of object with Frege's notion of reference. (i) In Frege the reference is an extralinguistic entity that the expression picks out, (ii) In Frege the reference is a real entity in the world. On the contrary, (iii) Husserl's notion of sense is not linguistic in character and it has to be understood from the point of view of the phenomenological reduction. Let us see this point.

First, the phenomenological reduction is essential to grasping the noema, in which is bracketing the existence of the world. Second, both noesis and noema belong (eidetically) to each other, that is to say, to understand the noema implies to understand the noesis, that is to say, in the analysis of the noema the phenomenologist has to include the study of the noesis as a result of the principle of the *a priori* correlation between noesis and noema. This rules out the linguistic interpretation of the noema as sense.

3. Immanence and Transcendence in the Structure Noesis and Noema

Until now we were considering the notion of noema as

synonymous to meaning, and this is only partly true, but in reality noema is equivalent to intentional object. Everything that is the intentional terminus of a conscious act is a noema.

As we saw in the last section, there are several concepts of immanent and transcendent in Husserl, which we have to clarify. The notions of immanent and transcendent are mutually exclusive, but we can find several levels of transcendence and immanence that overlap each other. These different levels of immanence and the corresponding transcendence have to be understood taking into consideration: (i) Every intentional act (noesis or *cogito*) has the characteristic of intentionality by which it is directed to an intentional object (noema or *cogitatum*); (ii) in the side of the noema or intentional object we have to distinguish between (a) what is immediately given, (b) what can be given in the succession of time, but is implied in what is immediately given, and (c) the thing in itself, which is not given but partially, in sides or adumbrations. Thus, we can distinguish these three levels of immanence and the corresponding transcendence:

(1) *Immanence as noesis and transcendence as noema.* The intentional act and its ingredients are the area of immanence, and everything belonging to the noema is transcendent to consciousness. For example, the intentional act of perceiving an apple tree is immanent, while the intentional object apple tree is transcendent. The criterion to distinguish what is immanent or transcendent is whether or not something is an integral part of the act of consciousness. Obviously, the intentional object is not an integral part of the act of consciousness, and because of this, it is transcendent to consciousness.

(2) *Immanence as noesis and what is immediately given in the noema, and transcendence as what is not immediately given in the noema.* For example, the intentional act of perceiving an apple tree and the eidos of the apple tree are immanent, but the future and the past of the apple tree are only implications. The past and the future are not present originally, in person. In this sense, what is past is transcendent. Here, the criterion for immanence and transcendence is what i given immediately and originally and what is not immediately and originally given, respectively.

(3) *Immanent is what is immediately given in the noema and its implications* (the past and the future). In this sense, the intentional act of perception, the intentional object apple tree, its past and future, are immanent to consciousness, but not the real and extramental apple tree in the natural world, which is transcendent to consciousness. Here the criterion for distinguishing immanence and transcendence is what is

given in some way and what is not given in any way.

So, we have that the thing itself is the absolute transcendent because the object is only given partially (in the terminology of *Logical Investigations*, the object is inadequately given to consciousness), while the past and future, which do not appear immediately, are just relative transcendents. On the contrary, the noesis is the absolute immanent because it is given perfectly without sides, or in the terminology of *Logical Investigations*, the object is adequately given to consciousness. (In general, here I will use the correlation transcendence and immanence according to the third level.)

We can summarize these ideas in the following table:

Noesis (cogito, or intentional act with its ingredient parts)	**Noema** (Cogitatum or intentional object)		
	Immediately given	Implied in the immediately given	Thing in itself
Immanent (1)	Transcendence (1)		
Immanent (2)	Transcendence (2)		
Immanent (3)	Transcendent (3)		

4. The Notion of Phenomenological Constitution of the Object

We know that phenomenology studies the immanency (third level of immanence) of consciousness, its subjective sphere, which embraces the *cogito* (the noesis, experience or mental act), the *cogitatum* (the noema, intentional object, etc.), and the ego. The effect of the *epoché* is to neutralize the natural tendency to go beyond the experience itself. In this way, I direct my attention to the experience I have of the things and the world, in a nutshell, to my subjectivity. Phenomenology does not deal with reality but the experience of reality.

We also know that after the phenomenological reduction, the phenomenon contains the same characteristics as the real thing; nothing is missing but the existence (existence is not a phenomenological datum according to Husserl). Now, if all characteristics of the real

65

thing are found in the phenomenon, then all characteristics of what is transcendent are at the same time characteristics of the immanence (third level of immanence) of consciousness. One who is familiar with Schopenhauer's philosophy would say that everything the world has is contained in the representation of the world.

From here we have that what the *epoché* does is simply to place into brackets what was a hypostasis, that is to say, (i) to place outside our experience something that belongs to our experience, or (ii) to make something independent when in reality it was dependent on my experience. Thus, the reality given in my experience is relocated in (reduced to) the experience of this reality. In conclusion, the reality, that the transcendency placed into brackets cannot be but the experience that one can have of it.

Having said this, a question arises, does reality lose its independent character from consciousness? Does phenomenology become a traditional idealism? These questions are difficult to resolve because technically there is neither "yes" nor "no" as an answer. It is "yes" as far as reality depends on a transcendental and intersubjective ego, but it is "no" as far as reality is more than the actual experience I have of it. As we will see later, reality is the totality of all actual and possible experiences of my ego and other egos. This is what Hussel calls "Phenomenological-transcendental idealism."

In this phenomenological context, reality is just the experience of reality. A step further in understanding the meaning of experience of reality is the notion of constitution,[10] which clarifies the meaning of transcendental reduction. With the use of the notion of constitution, Husserl can say that the ego constitutes its objects. So, we have here a constituing consciousness, a concept that we already used earlier.

A thing, as far as it is the object of a perception, is the unity to which all my actual and possible experiences refer. When I perceive a tree, I see only a side of the tree, a perspective. Now, to have this unity I need a scheme in which all possible experiences are anticipated. For example, to know that this is a tree I have to constitute the scheme of all possible experiences belonging to this object. The unity of different perspectives and sides of the tree is ruled by a scheme of familiarity that I constitute.

These schemes of familiarity have a genesis, an originary foundation (*Urstiftung*). The originary foundation of a scheme of familiarity is the learning of an originary knowledge (*ursprüngliches Kennenlernen*). Our consciousness learns progressively by constituting these schemes of familiarity, which determine the frame for the actual and possible experiences of the object in question.

As we will see later, the living consciousness is the ego with the totality of habits of these schemes. Schemes manifest a habituality to organize our experiences and constitute the scheme in which we experience any object.

The world as the conterpole of our subjectivity is constituted in our subjectivity. We can say with Husserl that to have a synoptic view of the totality of my life is like having a synoptic view of the totality of the world, and vice versa.

5. Formal and Transcendental Logic

5.1. Pure Logic as a Phenomenological Logic

Husserl maintains that because most of the logicians have not studied the connection between logic and the world, between logic and the experience, logic did not achieve its status of purity (independence from experience). Even more, most of the logicians were involved in a logic that implicitly presupposed a world (in the fashion of a positivistic science). This logic and all positivistic sciences are, from the point of view of phenomenology, constituted by the subject, but this constitution is not recognized by the subject as doing so (they are living in the natural attitude). If we want to gain purity in logic, we must analyze the level of logic that presupposes the world, and all positivistic sciences (which are concerned with the world), so that we can go beyond them to recover a genuine pure logic in which the word is no longer presupposed. This must be achieved by means of the phenomenological method.

Husserl is saying that traditional logic has not achieved the scientifc status of pure logic, and now he will provide that honorable status after the phenomenological reduction.[11]

Husserl attempts to make explicit that the world is implicit in the meaning of traditional logic. That is to say, in the terminology of phenomenology, Husserl attempts to uncover the presuppositions implicit in traditional logic. Husserl accomplishes this task in *Formal and Transcendental Logic*, where he studies the historical development of logic. It is here where Husserl discovers that Aristotle was the first philosopher who understood logic in its purity.

Aristotle established logic as the science of the assertive predicative judgement (what is called technically *apophansis*). Husserl notes that Aristotle used letters to stand for the cores of judgements (this is especially clear in his theory of syllogism), suggesting an intention for the purity and neutrality of logic.[12] Husserl develops this Aristotelian idea of purity and neutrality in logic according to the phenomenological method.

According to the phenomenological reduction, the grounds for any notion (here the notions of the science of logic) must be located in one's experience. Justification of a notion in a phenomenological context is achieved by isolating and reflecting on the *cogito* (and as a consequence, reflecting on the structure *ego cogito cogitatum*) that gives rise to the notion in question. The description of the structure *ego cogito cogitatum*, in which the notion is framed, yields deeply hidden subjective forms. In these subjective forms the theoretical reason brings about its productions.[13] Thus, justification of a notion is the recreating of the originary experience. To recreate the originary experience is not a mere repetition of the experience, but having the originary experience in a new form: one is now conscious that one is justifying. This is also called, by Husserl, clarification from the most original sources: a turning back to the intentionality that was the origin of the concept, or to put the concept back into the living intention of logicians.[14]

Now, we have a clear idea what is the difference between an objective formal logic and a phenomenological logic (or transcendental logic). The phenomenological logic grounds logical notions in subjective acts of experience, a procedure that Husserl considers indispensable to achieving the justification of a pure logic. On the contrary, an objective formal logic bases its justification on static objective concepts. Traditional logicians did not go further, and, maybe, the reason—Husserl suggests—was the fear of psychologism.[15] (As a matter of fact, Husserl tried to justify mathematical concepts in the *Philosophy of Arithmetic* in a way that resembles what he was doing in *Formal and Transcendental Logic*, although in a very imperfect way, and it was interpreted as psychologism by Frege, as we saw in the Chapter 2, Section 2). Husserl insisted vigorously that the method of justifying logical notions by going back to the subjectivity does not mean that it entails psychologism.

5.2. Pure Logic and Formal Ontology

One of the most interesting achievements of Husserl's analysis of pure logic is its extension to formal ontology. The notion of formal ontology is not only connected with pure logic but also with the intuition of essences and the idea of constitution. Here, I will give a very general idea that can suggest the scope of Husserl's intentions.

If we see formal logic from the point of view of its motivating idea—coming to know the object— then formal logic must consist not only of a formal theory of judgement, but it must include also a formal theory of the object, which Husserl calls "formal ontology." Husserl makes an illuminating comparison with mathematics. Pure mathematics is the science of the relations between any object whatever (relation of whole to part, relation of equality, property, unity, etc.). In this sense, pure mathematics is seen by Husserl as formal ontology.

The objects that formal ontology considers are categorial objects (see Chapter 2, Section 4.4.), and categorial objects are constituted in judgements. Categorial objects can be organized in regions, which give rise to different regional formal ontologies. In other words, we have here an *a priori* formal ontology that establishes all possible objects a science can deal with, and in general, a formal ontology is a theory of possible forms of theories.[16] Let us look at this with more detail.

Objects as phenomena for consciousness are constituted, that is to say, they are counter-poles of our subjective life. As we saw, every object or phenomenon has its specific mode of experience, where the phenomenon is constituted. From here, we have that objects belonging to a certain kind are counter-poles of experiences of a certain kind as well. Material objects are grasped by a type of experience; mathematical objects are grasped by another type of experience; and so on. Husserl calls "a region of being" these objects that are grasped by a kind of experience. There is a science that studies the essential characteristics of a region of being. The justification of this science is brought about by what Husserl calls "regional ontology." For example, a regional ontology determines what is the object that a science studies, how this object is given in the experience, which experiences of the object one can or cannot have. In other words, the aim of a regional ontology is to manifest the essence of the objects given to certain experiences. This essence, obviously, will mark the limits and possibilities of the science regulated under a regional ontology.

In order to manifest the essence of an object, we saw that Husserl exercises the eidetic reduction. This reduction must manifest that the object has a certain essential structure, without which the object would not be *that* object. Notice that the regional ontologies are not a substitution of any science. A regional ontology just wants to indicate the necessary requirements, *the (a priori) necessary conditions* of the science that falls under a certain regional ontology.

6. Theory of Ego: Egology

6.1. The Pure Ego

Husserl's doctrine of the pure ego is of high complexity and richness of phenomenological description and accuracy, with a very precise technical language that is necessary to keep to avoid confusion. The difficulties in a first reading are evident, and sometimes unavoidable.

Husserl distinguishes two sorts of egos or subjects of experience, the psychological ego and the pure ego. The psychological ego is a reality of the world, and the pure ego is a result of transcendental reduction, the *residuum* after exercising the *epoché* on the sphere of consciousness. This distinction has the consequence of stressing even more the separation between phenomenology, which is concerned with the pure ego, and psychology. However, this separation is not absolute in both directions, for psychology depends on phenomenology.

Husserl describes the pure ego as the pole from which all thinking is a ray. The ego radiates through its own acts. The pure ego is neither an intentional act nor an object but it reveals itself as an ego-pole that accompanies all my presentations, and penetrates them with its gaze without altering the situation. Two points deserve some clarification:

(1) *The pure ego is not an object*, and as a consequence is not properly a phenomenon. When I exercise a phenomenological reflection on the main structure of my consciousness "*ego cogito cogitatum*," the ego which is the object of my attention is not identical to the ego that is executing the phenomenological reflection. The ego escapes a complete thematization; it does not allow itself to become a complete object. It hides in the back of every reflection as the absolute subjective pole. The ego is not strictly a phenomenon but it is the a priori condition for any phenomenon, any object.

(2) The expression "without altering the situation" means that the experience or intentional act maintains the intention to its corresponding object while the ego accompanies the experience. One has to contrast this with the problem of self-observation posed by Brentano. In the self-observation of my mental act of anger, for example, the act of anger fades in favor of the new act of self-observation. If I want to observe my anger, necessarily the experience of anger looses its intensity and becomes a memory of anger, which is already another experience different from the original experience of

anger. This does not happen with the ego's gaze accompanying any mental act.

Because the pure ego is not an object or phenomenon, Husserl calls it the irreducible *residuum* of the *epoché*. It is always present in all mental activity, even during the performance of the *epoché*. In this sense, the pure ego is a transcendental (in the sense that Kant calls "transcendental") that accompanies all our conscious activities; the pure ego is a transcendental ego.

The ego is grasped in reflection (or inner perception) as the identity of the reflecting and the reflected: in inner perception I realize that what is reflected on is the same as the "I" who exercises the reflection. Nevertheless, in contrast with Kant, this identity of the ego is not merely logical because of the *temporality* of this identity. This idea of the temporality of the pure ego is the starting point from which Husserl maintains that the ego constitutes itself. Husserl maintain that the pure ego is the unity of immanent time with which it constitutes itself. *The pure ego is the identity of immanent time.* We can say that the ego certainly occurs, although it does not occur like a physical or psychical event. Maybe, the best way to understand this difficult question is to realize that the ego does not happen as an event does; rather, after the transcendental reduction, *everything that happens happens to the ego.* After the phenomenological reduction, if something happens, it happens as a phenomenon for my consciousness, but the ego is immune to this happening. Moreover, the identity of the ego is not the identity of an object like a tree under different sides. The pure ego does not appear at all as a phenomenon. Husserl claims that the pure ego is absolute selfhood: "[the pure ego] is given, rather, in absolute selfhood and in its unadumbratable unity and it is to be grasped adequately in reflection upon itself as a functional center in an adequate insight. As pure ego it conceals no hidden internal domain; it is absolutely simple and lies entirely open."[17]

After the *epoché*, the pure ego is non-real, but it is still a living (*Erlebnis*) subjectivity. This means that it has what Husserl calls "habitualities." Habitualities are not the real dispositions that psychologists attribute to the real ego. Habitualities are habits or manners of behaving of the pure ego. To put it in a more technical way, habitualities of the pure ego are a necessary structure of immanent time by which every mental operation (opinion, presentation, judgement, affection, etc.), is in such a way that its intentional object can be recognized in its permanence. The question here is not the recognition of a noematic identity, to recognize the same intentional object, but the recognition of myself as remaining in the same intentional process. In other words, it is the durable myself (the ego) that I rediscover and recognize. These habitualities are the permanence of an intentional act intending its object. In this sense, habitualities of the pure ego indicate the inclination from being to having,[18] or more specifically, from the me (being) to the mine (having). Husserl describes the habitualities as emerging from the self-constitution of the original time.

6.2. The Ego as a Monad

The idea of ego as a monad is taken from Leibniz's idea of monad as a dynamic center of integration. Husserl accepts this Leibnizian idea into the center of phenomenology. Husserl's notion of monad expresses a complete integration of every intentional presence into its sense, and every sense into the intentional acts, the *cogitationes* which intend or give the sense, and, finally, every intentional act, every *cogitatio* is integrated into the ego. Thus, Husserl expresses how everything as a phenomenon is the life of the ego. To be "the life of the ego" means that every phenomenon is *for me*; I, me, my ego, lives in every *cogitatio*, and through every *cogitatio*, I live in the sense or meaning that the cogitatio gives, and in the presence of every phenomenon given to me. The "for-me" of any phenomenon is unfolded from the ego.

In this picture, the habitualities of the life of the ego are at stake. The habits of the ego plays a mediating role between the world (after the reduction) and my living ego. The habitualities joins the world to my ego in an organic manner. From here, Husserl claims that "the concretion of the ego" (what can be called the complete ego, its whole life) is me, as an identical pole, plus my habitualities, plus my world. It is now obvious that this notion of monad marks the absolute relevance of interiority over exteriority (Husserl sides with Augustinian interiorism), and it marks, too, the priority of the transcendental over the transcendent (Husserl sides with Kant's transcendental philosophy).

Let us look at the idea of the ego as the identical pole. In the *Cartesian Meditations* (Fourth Meditation) Husserl takes on the task of reducing all preceding intentional analysis up into the ego, that is to say, to insert the acts of the ego back into the ego. Husserl notices that the ego is not an object; it is not a strict phenomenon, but a phenomenon is always something for me, while *the ego is something for itself*. The ego does not appear to me as a phenomenon appears; the ego is what it is for itself. From here, Husserl makes an important

72

observation justified in the pure description of consciousness: the character of "for-me" of every phenomenon (the world, its objects, etc. as far as they are phenomenological reduced) does not exhaust the character of "for-itself" of the ego. The descriptive reason is that the ego is "for itself" means that *the ego constitutes itself*. This egological constitution involves several steps:

(1) *The ego is the identical pole of the multiplicity of mental acts*. The manifold of cogitations has a unique subjective pole. The ego is, then, the identical me which lives actively or passively in the subjective processes of consciousness (mental acts), and through them, relates to intentional objects as the counter-poles.[19] It is interesting to notice that the *cogitata* or noemata (the intentional objects) are the correlates of both the manifold *cogitationes* (mental acts) and of the identical ego; this is a result of the descriptive fact that the ego lives in the *cogitata* (noemata) "through" the *cogitations*.

(2) Now, *the ego is not only the reference pole but it is also the substratum of permanent properties*. (Later, Husserl justifies the character of person based on these permanent properties.) The ego is a subject of habitualities. The ego is in relation to its habitualities as being and having. What is interesting in these ideas is that "having" is an originary structure of transcendental experience. The ego "has" habitualities, and by the habits the ego, me, inhabits "my" world.

(3) Thus, we arrive to the constitution of the ego as the identical pole by which its habitualities inhabit the world. We have the following equation of the concretion of the ego:

Concretion of the ego = me as identical pole + habitualities as the havings of the ego + my world as reduced

7. Solipsism and Intersubjectivity

7.1. The Idea of Phenomenological Idealism

The program of *Ideas Pertaining to a Pure Phenomenology and a Phenomenological Philosophy* was developed in *First Philosophy*, volume II, which is dedicated to the theory of the phenomenological reduction. This work ends in the thesis of phenomenological idealism as the result of the method of the phenomenological reduction. This sort of idealism is different from the classical idealism. The latter is a metaphysical thesis, which the phenomenological reduction put out of action. On the contrary, phenomenological idealism is a methodical position open to intersubjectivity as a result of what Husserl calls "double reduction," and, in turn, the discovery of intersubjectivity ends in a phenomenological universe of monads.

Let us see the meaning of phenomenological idealism for Husserl. According to our philosopher, the phenomenological idealism is not a thesis or another philosophical theory. If it were, phenomenology would betray itself. Precisely, the phenomenological reduction is to put out of action all theories; phenomenology only admits the principle of all principles, the principle of intuition, what is immediately given. Contrary to classical idealism, which is a metaphysical thesis, the phenomenological idealism does not reject the existence of the world but places it into brackets in order to reach a knowledge based on absolute evidence (the principle of intuition), which allows the building of a rigorous and presuppositionless science. The phenomenological point of view is that everything I know has to be a content of consciousness, a content of my experience. The phenomenological method consists of reducing our knowledge to this content of experience by putting out of action the natural thesis, the thesis that believes in the extramental existence of things. Husserl claims that even in the case of a supernatural revelation from God, this revelation cannot be given to us if it is not given as content of my own experience, and, as a consequence, it is subject to phenomenological reduction as well.[20] The phenomenologist is a universal spectator of what happens in the world and in the immanence of his consciousness.

Phenomenological idealism is the result of being this universal spectator who only pays attention to the evidence of what is immediately given in intuition. Everything is either a phenomenon for consciousness or its immanent origin (the pure ego). It is important to notice again that to be this universal spectator is an attitude and not a theory or a metaphysical thesis; it is the phenomenological attitude freely accepted.

7.2. The Problem of Solipsism

Solipsism is a term derived from the Latin *solus ipse*, meaning only me. Solipsism is a philosophical term that means that only the ego exists. In phenomenology, this idea derives from the isolation of Descartes' philosophy, in which the starting point of his philosophy, "I think therefore I exist," cannot allow him rigorously to exit from the immanence of consciousness, which implies a rejection of all that is transcendent to consciousness. All philosophies inspired in the Cartesian *cogito* have the problem of building a bridge (an impossible bridge?) from the starting point of consciousness to the external world. The result of this is the isolation and solitude of the very ego. There is no external world and there are no other egos; there is only the ego in its pure solitude. In general, solipsism is one of the possible effects, if not a side-effect, of any idealism. Phenomenology, as far as it is a form of idealism, is subject to solipsism.

The phenomenological solipsism is a result of the phenomenological reduction: everything I can experience, everything I can understand as true has to be an intentional content of my conscious life. Everything I can know has to be something for me (a phenomenon for me). It seems that everything is just a pure and simple intentional pole of my consciousness. The natural world is reduced to a phenomenon. Things existing in the world are filtered of their existence. Other egos, as far as they are things in the world, are also reduced to phenomena for me. It seems that the phenomenologist lives only with his ego, a life of solitude without other egos, a phenomenological solipsism. Nevertheless, Husserl rejects this view because it is possible to justify descriptively a phenomenology of the other, and, thus, to affirm a universe of egos. This is the subject of intersubjectivity.

7.3. The Experience of Other Egos

For Husserl there is another mode of consciousness that is as valid as the one he has been using so far. In addition to the priority of the principle of all principles —intuition of what is immediately given— there is another principle that is, in some way, derived from the former: empathy (*Einfühlung*) or experience of the other. Husserl believes that there is no danger of falling into solipsism because the *alter ego* (the other ego) presents itself to me through the living body. The *alter ego* is presented to me as another subjectivity and not as a mere phenomenon, a mere intentional pole of my consciousness.

This procedure implies that the phenomenological reduction leads us to two conscious lives which are mutually founded.[21] The impossibility of reducing the *alter ego* to a mere phenomenon or intentional pole is because Husserl is using a double reduction. He distinguishes in the experience of empathy two elements (i) the very act of consciousness and (ii) its content. The act of empathy is an act belonging to the conscious life as any other mental act, but the content —the *alter ego*— is not presented as a mere phenomenon for me. What is presented in the act of empathy is another consciousness, or better, another conscious ego. Now, as we saw before, the ego is not an object, it is not a mere phenomenon, it cannot be made a full phenomenon for me. If any conscious ego has this surprising descriptive characteristic, then the *alter ego* has to keep the same characteristics. It means that other conscious egos are presented by the act of empathy not as a mere intentional object but as a full living ego. In other words, the conscious empathy does not present mere phenomena but living egos.

This descriptive analysis implies that Husserl, for the first time, is allowed to exit the immanence of his own consciousness to admit the immanence of another consciousness, that is to say, to transcend his own immanent limits. The *alter ego* as the content of the empathy is not part (intentional part, noema) of consciousness, or as Husserl puts it, "the objective datum of empathy and the corresponding experience of empathy *cannot belong to the same stream of consciousness*, that is to say, to the same phenomenological ego."[22]

To clarify this difficult point better, Husserl has some important phenomenological considerations based on the phenomenological analysis of the time consciousness. The "now" of my mental act of empathy is originally different from the "now" of the other ego, which is playing the role of object of my empathy. Maybe my subjective now (not the objective now of physics) coincides with the other subjective now, but they are descriptively different. Any consciousness has its own phenomenological time, and the coincidence of both times is only reached by means of the objective time of both the body and the mundane things. So, the alter ego does not belong to the stream of my consciousness because of two different subjective times.

7.4. Intersubjectivity

The most difficult point that any phenomenologist finds in Husserl's phenomenology is the analysis of intersubjectivity. This analysis starts with the double reduction of the empathy, the constitution of the *alter ego*, and the constitution of the world and the universe of monads.

The most controversial and, at the same time, one of the most interesting Husserliam subject is the experience of the other ego by means of empathy. The whole problem can be summarized as follows: How can I recognize, within the pure limits of the phenomenological reduction, the distinction between my originary sphere and the other originary sphere. A presuppositionless science (phenomenology) with no ontological commitments seems to have trouble recognizing other egos as other originary centers like me. Is not this a surreptitious ontological commitment? Did not the *epoché* put out of action any object in the world, and as a consequence, other egos?

We saw how empathy can allow the recognition of an *alter ego*, but how is this possible? If empathy is an act of consciousness, and all acts are intentional in character, that is to say, they intend an intentional object, then, why is not the object of empathy an intentional object as the rest of the intentional acts? Why is the *alter ego* (object of the act of empathy) more than a mere intentional object? What Husserl calls "the constitution of the *alter ego*" is a highly complex process which is still under investigation. We can summarize this process in the following steps:

(1) Transcendental reduction of the ego by which the *epoché* is exercised in the domain of my own consciousness. Here I discover the mental acts of empathy, by which I realized the presence of other egos.

(2) The result of the act of empathy is a radical modification of the presentation of the other ego as *originally other*. In empathy I realize that the other ego is not like another object, it is like me, the center of constitution, the origin of intentionality.

(3) The empathy of the other ego acquires ontological status when it is presented embodied in a body. The empathy offers me the experience of another ego which is embodied and acts in its body.

(4) The experience of the other body is phenomenologically identical with other physical bodies, but I experience it analogically as a psychophysical body.

(5) From here, Husserl claims that in the experience of the other body there is an overlapping of the other originary sphere with mine. As we saw before, there is no confusion in this overlapping because of the different originary times of both conscious egos.

(6) As a result of the last step, my consciousness undergoes the effect of self-alienation or self-externalization (*Selbstentfremdung*), which is a projection of my originary conscious sphere into the living body of the other, or to take oneself as an Other. In other words, what Husserl means consists of externalizing one originary ego and its originary sphere as an Other's. And vice versa, in any *alter ego*, the originary conscious sphere undergoes the self-alienation into my living body.

(7) The mutual self-alienation gives rise to the multiplication of different originary conscious spheres or subjectivities. The result is a plurality of coexistent other egos, and among them I am experienced by others as an other. I am an *alter ego* for the other egos; this creates a community of mutual other egos.

According to Husserl, empathy arrives to this conclusion, that I am for me a subject, and all other egos are also for me a subject of originary acts (including the acts of empathy). We have here a phenomenological intersubjectivity. In summary, the phenomenological intersubjectivity is consciousness of its own subjectivity and another subjectivity. *Intersubjectivity is a mutual subjective internal perception (apperception).*

To better understand this conclusion, let us consider the following analysis. The ego is a pole with counter-poles (the intentional object), but this intentional object is not the opposite of the ego. What is properly the opposite of the ego is the *alter ego.*. If we understand the notion of opposition as something that has to be mutual and belong to the same category, then the ego can only be opposed to another ego.

7.5. Universe of Monads

The ego as a monad is an immanent life with an immanent time. Another ego implies another immanent life with another immanent time. The universe of the monads is the sum of all egos in mutual apperception (internal perception). I, as a monad, have the horizon of self-alienation (*Selbstentfremdung*) of other monads, and vice versa, and this constitutes the "us" as a universe of monads. *This "us" is what is properly called intersubjectivity, and in this intersubjectivity the world is constituted objectively.*

The world which is constituted in front of me is not the whole world. The latter is a result of a universe of monads. By means of the act of empathy, I know other egos, which have perceptions of the world. I notice these perceptions of other egos through empathy. From here, Husserl arrives to the conclusion that I become conscious that the object perceived by me and by another ego is the same object; and the same intersubjective process is reproduced in the other ego. Hence, a true objectivity for me is at the same time an objectivity for another ego. [23]

The phenomenological intersubjectivity is a community of egos in mutual coexistence, which is the universe of monads. This leads to what Husserl calls "transcendence in the immanence," that is to say, the fact that the *alter ego* (what is transcendent) appears in the intentional analysis of the originary sphere of the ego (what is immanent). More explicitly, the ego-monad is a concrete ego that embraces the actual and potential conscious life, the present, the future and the past, in addition to this temporal dimension, here is where the reference to alterity appears, the reference to the *alter ego* is present.

Consciousness after the process of phenomenological reduction is the only thing that maintains an absolute character while the world is relative to consciousness (this is the main subject-matter of *Ideas I*). Now, from the point of view of the phenomenological intersubjectivity, the totality of what is absolute is constituted by all phenomenological egos. This is what Husserl now calls "universe of monads." Thus, we see how Husserl's phenomenology arrives to the monadology, which Leibniz anticipated. Here there is an identification between phenomenological idealism (or transcendental phenomenology) with the monadology, but with an important difference from Leibniz's monadology, namely, Husserl's monadology is not metaphysical but phenomenological. The phenomenological monadology is a result of the description of consciousness, and it has nothing to do with a metaphysical construction. There is no construction or speculation, but only descriptive results from what is given in pure intuition. In other words, in the analysis of intentionality we find the foundation for the transcendence of other egos. In addition to this, for Leibniz, a monad does not have windows, that is to say, it does not communicate with other monads, they are incommunicable and isolated monads. On the contrary, for Husserl, monads have windows because they communicate with each other. The windows of the monads are the acts of empathy.

8. The Life-World

In Husserl's last published work in his life, *The Crisis of European Sciences and Transcendental Phenomenology*, he becomes more radical than in *Ideas I*. The *epoché* is applied now to the life-world (*Lebenswelt*.) This is the only supposition that was not taken thematically into consideration.

The *epoché* reduced the natural world to the world as a phenomenon for me. This new change of attitude (the phenomenological attitude) is a subjective change of the modes of being given, or forms of appearance of the world. The world appears as being for us. This phenomenon is what now has to be analyzed.

The science of the life-world is the science of the subjectivity as far as the world is a phenomenon for us, but with a new characteristic: the world is now presented in its pre-giveness (*Vorgegebenheit*), the sole ground from which all human activity is originated. This notion of world is the base for any objectivity. This means that science, politics, ethics, and in general, the human knowledge presuppose the pre-giveness of the world, which is the life-world.

To see the world with this new attitude is to see how the world acquires meaning and validity in the life of consciousness.[24] There is a reduction of the world to a transcendental phenomenon: the world is the universe of space-temporal things. In the natural attitude we find the interest in developing an ontology, and the sciences corresponding to the things in the natural world. The life of consciousness lives (experience) the world in constant certainty. Although things and the world form a unity because of the reciprocity in which one and the other is experienced: (i) things are given in the horizon of the world and the world is the totality of things; and (ii) I have consciousness of one in reference to the other and vice versa. Nevertheless, both things and the world are different in the manner of being given because the world is not an object or thing, but it has a peculiar manner of being given in which there is no plural. There is one world for many things.

The life-world is the noematic correlate of the intersubjective experience. A phenomenological description of the life-world must capture the horizon for physical, historical, social, aesthetic dimensions. Given the experience of intersubjectivity, the world is no longer my world but our world, and the ego is no longer a solitary ego but the transcendental "we." Husserl is adopting here an approach, which Wittgenstein introduced almost at the same time, the approach to a holistic point of view.

The main point of Husserl's notion of life-world is as follows: one must not go straight back to the supposedly immediately given sense data, as if they were immediately characteristic of the purely intuitive data of the life-world, rather, it is the holistic view of the life-world that is the only datum with which phenomenological analysis must begin. *We have a world pre-given* with its ontic meaning,[25] and each thing that we experience (even ourselves, our egos) gives itself, whether or not we notice, *as a thing in the world.* In every experience of a thing, the life-world is given as the *ultimate foundation of all objective knowledge.*[26] Thus, the life-world comprises the only foundation of all our philosophical, scientific, moral, and in general everyday mundane activity. Even more, physical objects, properties, facts, numbers, moral values, hyletic data, etc., are merely moments abstracted form the life-world, which plays the role of an *a priori* for any human activity. Husserl summarizes this by saying: "Science is a human spiritual accomplishment which presupposes as its point of departure ... the intuitive surrounding world of life, pre-given as existing for all in common."[27]

The everyday praxis determines the life-world, and both are the subsoil for every human activity, thinking, etc. It is not necessary that we are conscious of the "everyday practice" and the life-world it determines, they are usually unthinkably presupposed and taken for granted: "to live is always to live-in-certainty-of-the-world."[28]

The world as it is for us is understandable as a structure of meaning, which is formed out of elementary intentionalities. The most elementary of these intentionalities are those involved in the activities of the human living body. These activities receive the meaning only within the context of an intersubjective system of practice and values. Husserl thinks that *the task of phenomenology is to go back to the intentional origins of the formation of any meaning.* This is an attempt to understand the intersubjective constitution of the life-world, and how these inherited traditions and received practice function in it. There is here a historical background reflection that expresses the historical beings that we are.[29]

* * *

With his last work —*The Crisis*— Husserl modified his conception of phenomenology that had been present for thirty years. This modification is not a rectification but an enhancement from an ego-oriented phenomenology to an intersubjective oriented one, and finally to a holistic view, in which the sole datum of departure of phenomenology is the life-world. Perhaps the most important modification of Husserl's phenomenology is the idea of a rigorous science, which lasted for many years, and after writing his last work (*The Crisis*) he thought that that idea was not exact any more: "Philosophy as science, as serious, rigorous, indeed apodictically rigorous science — the dream is over."[30] I do not think that Husserl rejected the idea as a rigorous science, but it is integrated in the new view of life-world, something that he did not have the time to develop.

ENDNOTES

[1] Edmund Husserl, *The Crisis of European Sciences and Transcendental Phenomenology*, translated by David Carr, Evanston, Northwestern University Press, 1970. Appendix III.
[2] Edmund Husserl, *Cartesian Meditations*, translated by D. Cairns, The Hague, Nijhoff, 1973, I, § 3.
[3] Husserl, *Ideas I*, § 34.
[4] Cf. Husserl, *Ideas I*, § 88.

[5] Cf. Husserl, *Ideas I*, § 86.
[6] Cf. Husserl, *Crisis*, § 41.
[7] Husserl, *Ideas I*, § 98.
[8] Husserl, *Ideas I*, § 131.
[9] Husserl, *Ideas I*, § 129.
[10] Before Husserl, Kant used this notion in the *Critique of Pure Reason*.
[11] Cf. Edmund Husserl, *Formal and Transcendental Logic*, trans. by Dorion Cairns, The Hague, Martinus Nijhoff, 1969, 289-330.
[12] Cf. Husserl, *Formal and Transcendental Logic*, pp. 42-43.
[13] Cf. Husserl, *Formal and Transcendental Logic*, p. 30.
[14] Cf. Husserl, *Formal and Transcendental Logic*, p. 9.
[15] Cf. Husserl, *Formal and Transcendental Logic*, p.183.
[16] Cf. Husserl, *Formal and Transcendental Logic*, p.79.
[17] Husserl, *Ideas pertaining to a Pure Phenomenology and to a Phenomenological Philosophy*, second book, translated by R. Rojcewicz and A. Schuwer, Dordrecht, Kluwer Academic Publishers, 1993, § 25 (Quoted as *Ideas II*).
[18] Cf. Husserl, *Ideas II*, § 29.
[19] Cf. Husserl, *Cartesian Meditations*, II, § 21.
[20] Cf. Edmund Husserl, *Erste Philosophie. Erste Teil: Kritishe Ideengeschichte*, R. Boehm (ed.), 1956, *Husserliana, - Edmund Husserl, Gerammelte WErke*, The Hague, Nijhoff, vol. VII, II, 182-183.
[21] Cf. Husserl, *Erste Philosophy I*, p. 188.
[22] Husserl, *Erste Philosophy I*, p.189.
[23] Cf. Edmund Husserl, *Erste Philosophie. Zweiter Teil: Theory der phänomenologische n Reduktion*, R. Boehm (ed.), 1959, *Husserliana, - Edmund Husserl, Gerammelte WErke*, The Hague, Nijhoff, vol. VIII, § 54, p. 190.
[24] Cf. Husserl, *Crisis*, § 39.
[25] Cf. Husserl, *Crisis*, § 28.
[26] Cf. Husserl, *Crisis*, § 66.
[27] Husserl, *Crisis*, § 33.
[28] Husserl, *Crisis*, § 37.
[29] Cf. Husserl, *Crisis*, § 15.
[30] Husserl, *Crisis*, Appendix IX, p. 389.

Bibliography

1. Major Writings of Husserl

The main source for the writings of Husserl were published in *Husserliana - Edmund Husserl, Gesammelte Werke*, The Hague: Nijhoff, 1950ff in 27 volumes by the Husserl Archives in Louvain under the direction of Professor H. L. Van Breda.

Some of the major writings of Husserl published in English:

Logical Investigations, trans. by J.N. Findlay, London, Routledge & Kegan Paul, 1970.

The Idea of Phenomenology, trans. by W.P. Alston and G. Nakhnikian, The Hague, Nijhoff, 1964.

Cartesian Meditations, trans. by D. Cairns, The Hague, Nijhoff, 1973.

Ideas Pertaining to a Pure Phenomenology and to a Phenomenological Philosophy, trans. by F. Kersten, The Hague, Nijhoff, 1982 (First Book)

Ideas Pertaining to a Pure Phenomenology and to a Phenomenological Philosophy, trans. by R. Rojcewics and A. Schuwer, The Hague, Nijhoff, 1989 (Second Book)

The Phenomenology of Internal Time-Consciousness, trans. by J.S. Churchill, Bloomington, Indiana University Press, 1964.

"Philosophy as Rigorous Science" in *Phenomenology and the Crisis of Philosophy*, trans. by Quentin Lauer, New York, Harper & Row, 1965.

Formal and Transcendental Logic, trans. by D. Cairns, The Hague, Nijhoff, 1969.

The Crisis of European Sciences and Transcendental Philosophy, trans. by D. Carr, Evanston, Northwestern University Press, 1970.

Experience and Judgement. Investigations in a Genealogy of Logic, trans. by J.S. Churchill and K. Ameriks, London, Routledge & Kegan Paul, 1973.

2. Selection of Works on Husserl's Philosophy

Bachelard, S., *A Study of Husserl's Formal and Transcendental Logic*, trans. by L.E. Embree, Evanston, Northwestern University Press, 1968.

Bell, David, *Husserl*, London, Routledge, 1990.

Bernet, Rudolf, Kern, Iso and Morbach, Eduardo, *An Introduction to Husserlian Phenomenology*, Evanston, Northwestern University Press, 1993.

Cairns, Dorion, *Conversations with Husserl and Fink*, The Hague, Martinus Nijhoff, 1976.

De Boer, Th., *The Development of Husserl's Thought*, trans. by T. Plantinga, The Hague, Nijhoff, 1978.

Elliston, F. and McCornick, Peter (eds.), *Husserl. Expositions and Appraisals*, Notre Dame, University of Notre Dame, 1977.

Farber, Marvin, *The Aims of Phenomenology. The Motives, Methods, and Impact of Husserl's Thought*, New York, Harper, 1966.
The Foundations of Phenomenolgy, Cambridge (Mass.), Harvard University Press, 1943.

Føllesdal, Dreyfus, *Husserl and Frege*, Oslo, Aschehoug, 1958.

Gurwitsch, A., *The Field of Consciousness*, Pittsburg, Duquesne University Press, 1964.

Ingarden, R., *On the Motives which Led Husserl to Transcendental Idealism*, tran. by A. Hannibalson, The Hague, Nijhoff, 1976.

Levinas, Emmanuel, *The Theory of Intuition in Husserl's Phenomenology*, trans. by André Orianne, Evanston, Northwestern University Press, 1973.

McKenna, W., Harlan, R. M. and Winters, L.E. (eds), *A Priori and Worl. European Contribution to Husserlian Phenomenology*, The Hague, Nijhoff, 1981.

Mensch, James R., Intersubjectivity and Transcendental Idealism, Albany, State University of New York Press, 1995.

Muralt, André de, *The Idea of Phenomenology: Husserlian Exemplarism*, transl. by Garry L. Breckon, Evanston, Northwestern University Press, 1974.

Osborn, Andrew D., *Edmund Husserl and His Logical Investigations*, 2nd ed., Cambridge (Mass.), 1949.

Ricoeur, Paul, *Husserl. An Analysis of His Phenomenology*, Evanston, Northerwestern University Press, 1967.

Sallis, John (ed.), *Husserl and Contemporary Thought*, Atlantic Highlands, Humanities Press, 1983.

Seifert, Josef, *Back to Things in Themselves. A Phenomenological Foundation for Classical Realism*, New York, Routledge & Kegan Paul, 1987.

Sokolowski, Robert., *The Formation of Husserl's Concept of Constitution*, The Hague, Nijhoff, 1964.
Husserlian Meditations: How Words Present Things, Evanston,

Northwestern University Press, 1974.
Spiegelberg, Herbert, *The Phenomenological Movement: A Historical Introduction*, vols, I and II, The Hague, Nijhoff, 1960.
  Phenomenology in Psychology and Psychiatry, Evanston, Northwestern University Press, 1972.
Tito, Johana Maria, *Logic in The Husserlian Context*, Evanston, Northwestern University Press, 1990.